AF417489

*Knowing one's place in a world
in search of reference points*

Agossou Arthur VIDO

Knowing one's place in a world in search of reference points

Essay for a restoration of African identities

Preface by Justin T. AVOLONTO

KONDO PRESS
The complete horizon of African knowledge

© **A. A. Vido** & **Kondo Press,** Minneapolis, 2026
Site: www.kondopress.com
Email: info@kondopress.com
Tel: +1 (763) 202-8400
Minneapolis, Minnesota (USA)
Address: 202 N Cedar Ave Ste #1, Owatonna, MN 55060 US

Photo, graphic design and layout: Wanilo Bertrand Ananou

ISBN: 979-8-90449-000-3

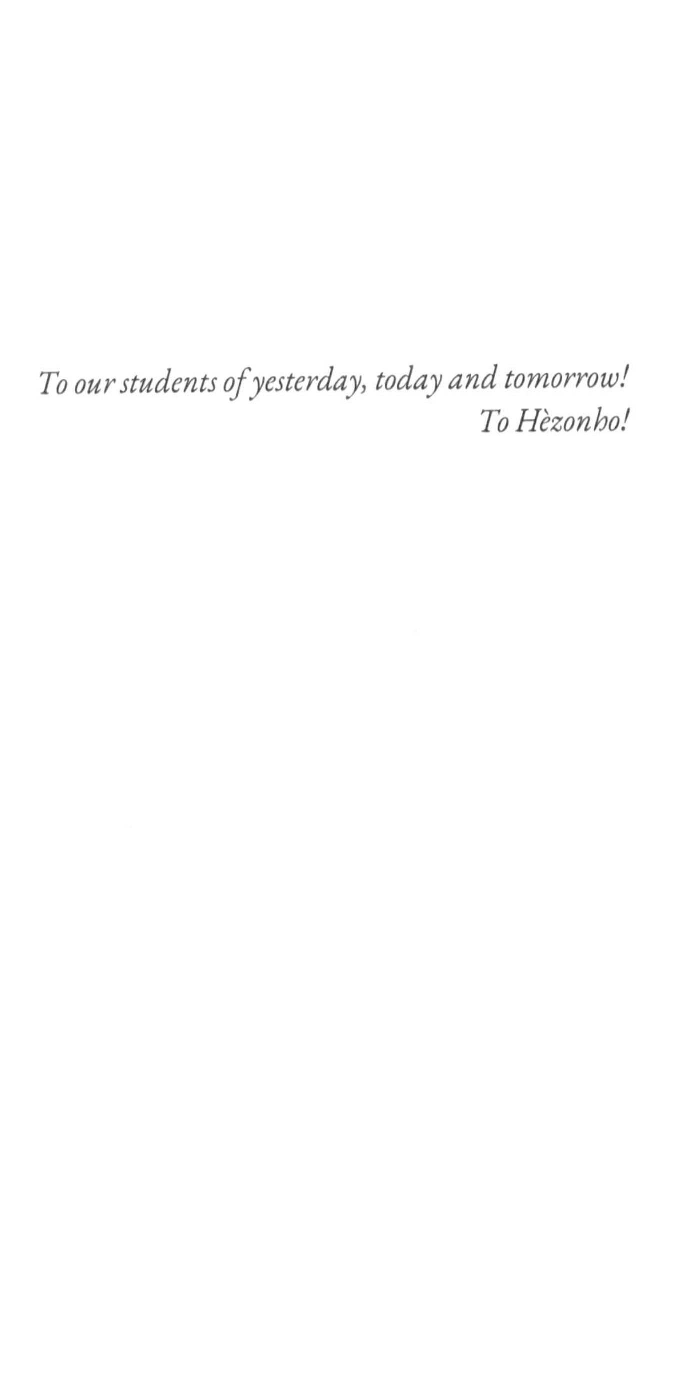

To our students of yesterday, today and tomorrow!
To Hèzonho!

"Colonialism has led us to doubt ourselves to such an extent that Africa has become, at a subconscious level, antithetical to the notion of civilisation (...) Humanity was born in Africa".

Cheikh Anta Diop (1983).

"There is an awesome power in books. Every word, every sentence in them has the potential to transform our lives, enabling us to move from complete ignorance to clear understanding, or from established knowledge to an achievement of unparalleled magnitude. There is power in books, let's learn to use it and channel it".

A. A. V.

Preface

M r. Agossou Arthur Vido has done me the honor of requesting a preface for his book, slated for publication in April 2026, and it is with profound joy and respect for this scientist that I shall provide an overview of his intellectual trajectory and his latest publication.

Decidedly! The publication of a book by Agossou Arthur Vido has become a recurring event. The only proof I have is the importance and number of works written by this author over the past eight years. To my knowledge, the author concerned has published, co-published, edited and co-edited 23 books during this period, including two books in 2025, three in 2024, two in 2023, four in 2022, two in 2021, three in 2020, four in 2019 and three in 2018. Moreover I am certain that I did not succeed in procuring all the works written by him during the aforementioned period. Today, the second book marking Agossou Arthur Vido's 2026 publications is entitled ***Knowing one's place in a world in search of reference points. Essay for a restoration of African identities***.

Far from answering only one question, this book responds to an urgent need. Indeed, in a global context marked by identity confusion, the massive circulation of unverified information and the persistence of stereotypes inherited from centuries of dominating ideologies, the question of Africa's place in universal history remains central. Moreover, the way Africans represent themselves appears as a decisive issue for the future of the continent. It is to this fundamental question that the author makes a major contribution here.

This work proceed neither from a simple academic exercise nor a polemical intent. It arises from a profound pedagogical encounter: a question posed by of a student, who is also African, asking if Africans would be "cursed". Behind this questioning reveals a silent wound, an interiorized doubt, a mental heritage shaped by centuries of theological, colonial and racial discourse. The author could have been content with a brief response. He chose the most demanding path: that of in-depth research, scientific rigor and structured knowledge transmission. This book is therefore primarily an act of teaching. It is the natural extension of an assumed intellectual responsibility. In fact, according to Cheikh Anta Diop, it represents an act of "recovering African cultural heritage".

The originality of this work lies in its method. The author does not merely assert; he demonstrates. He questions sources, confronts texts and mobilizes biblical traditions as well as Arabo-Muslim writings, the works of contemporary historians, anthropological research and scientific data related to the origins of humanity. The myth of the "curse of Ham", often invoked to justify the enslavement of African people, is subjected to meticulous critical examination.

The analysis of Genesis, the contextualization of medieval and modern interpretations, and the exposure of theological instrumentalizations sufficiently demonstrate the lack of any foundation for such a racial theory in the Holy Scriptures. Through this approach, the author follows in the footsteps of great African thinkers such as Cheikh Anta Diop or Wole Soyinka, Aimé Césaire or Théophile Obenga, who worked to restore Africa's historical depth and intellectual dignity, without complacency or victimization.

Furthermore, Agossou Arthur Vido goes beyong deconstructing a myth; he reconstructs a memory by advocating for the restoration of identities through knowledge. One of the essential merits of this work is its articulation of a critique of prejudice alongside an appreciation of African contributions to universal history: as the cradle of humanity, a site for the domestication of useful plants, and a hub for scientific development in medicine, in mathematics and in other disciplines. In recalling these realities, the author does not seek to glorify the past naively. He adopts the posture of a man of science: recognizing greatness without concealing weaknesses, affirm contributions without denying contemporary challenges. It is less a matter of exaltation than of restoration. In a world in search of landmarks, knowing one's place does not mean isolating oneself. It means understanding where one comes from to better participate in the universal dialogue.

Consequently, this book is addressed to all categories of literati, even if it speaks with a particular intensity to the students, to the young researchers. He offers them intellectual tools to think for themselves. He invites them to leave fatalistic explanations and to substitute the method for emotion. In this, the book participates in a fundamental mission: to train critical minds capable of assuming their heritage without inferiority complexes or temptation to self-glorify. The author implicitly recalls that true emancipation arises neither from permanent complaint nor from a noisy claim, but from mastery of knowledge.

Mr. Agossou Arthur Vido does not write as a distant observer. An Associate Professor (CAMES), he is the Deputy Head of the Department of History and

Archaeology at the University of Abomey-Calavi in Benin. As a Teacher-Researcher, he writes as a pedagogue, a historian, and a researcher committed to cultivating an enlightened consciousness. Its research activity in archives, as well as in national and international libraries, and its use of diverse sources, illustrate a permanent commitment to scientific credibility. Her approach is marked by serenity and rigor; he eschews stigmatization, avoids invective and prioritizes argumentation. This stance gives the work a particular strength: that of quiet reason. By eschewing the quest for external validation, Agossou Arthur Vido asserts an intellectual sovereignty that aligns him once more with the legacy of the illustrious Cheikh Anta Diop, who addressed African intellectuals on December 7, 1972: "It is a matter of being able to discover scientific truth by one's own means, without the approval of others, and thus knowing how to maintain one's intellectual autonomy [...] Competence becomes the supreme virtue of the African who wants to disalienate his people".

The work of Agossou Arthur Vido is a necessary contribution to our time. At a time when social networks amplify simplifying narratives and where identities are fragmenting, this essay recalls an essential truth: history is not a weapon of condemnation, but an instrument of understanding. The alleged curse of the Black Man, accurately dismantled in these pages, appears for what it is: an ideological construction. Against this, the author opposes the patience of research, the solidity of the sources and the coherence of the analysis.

This work is not only a plea; it is an invitation,
Invitation to know
Invitation to reflect
Invitation to stand.

It will undoubtedly contribute to nourishing academic debates, enriching university libraries and enlightening the consciences of those who are looking for solid references in a world traversed by uncertainties.

May the readers — students of yesterday, today and tomorrow — find in these pages not only answers but also the intellectual courage to fully assume their place in the common history of humanity. "It is in this way [said Cheikh Anta Diop] that scientific thought will be put at the service of Africa as effectively as possible".

My sincere deference to the author.

Cotonou, March 13, 2026.

Doctor Justin T. AVOLONTO
Historian,
Assistant Professor (CAMES)
African Retrospective Research Laboratory
(LabRA) /UAC.

Introduction

During the 2022-2023 academic year, in a course held from 7 a.m. to 10 a.m. entitled History of Science and Technology, we explained to the students that medicine and agriculture were, among other things, practices specific to Africa, without external influences. After the presentation, as we invited the second-year students to express their concerns about the chapter, one of them asked us the following question: "Mr Vido, do you think that we Africans are cursed?".

With the calmness required by the situation, we replied: ''Sir, I don't think so! History, which is a serious and well-established discipline, has already shown that!''. Following this reply, the student paused, revealing a certain dissatisfaction. He was right, the answer was rather succinct! We then went on to explain that, in the light of current historical data, everything points to the fact that the African is not the object of a curse issued by Noah, a patriarch mentioned in the Bible, particularly in the book of Genesis.

To the student who seemed very preoccupied by the subject, we promised to send him some documents during the next lesson scheduled for the following week. We kept our promise, and both he and the other students present were given materials, both digital and physical, to help them properly understand the subject of the supposed curse of the Black Man. That day, we realised that the subject, which we thought had been widely debated and had now been assimilated by Africans, was still the subject of long debates, often punctuated by astonishing misunderstandings. In the course of our discussions with other second and third year history students, we discovered that many believed that the so-called curse of the African was a tangible reality, explaining the underdevelopment in various areas of the continent[1].

It is true that, during his speech on 26 July 2007 at Cheikh Anta Diop University in Dakar, Senegal, Nicolas Sarkozy, then President of the French Re-

---

[1] We wish to reassure the reader that the reality described by our students does not reflect in any way the opinion expressed by the majority.

public, on his first official visit to sub-Saharan Africa, described the Black Man as relatively detached from his own history, subtly trying to make him accept the ''congenital incapacity of his race[2] ''. On this basis, the statesman sometimes posed as a father figure or guardian addressing his children, sometimes as a missionary believing himself to be the bearer of a saving message. However, in response to the shocking and condescending nature of the discourse, on 11 September 2007 the Malian historian Adame Ba Konaré launched an appeal to academics, inviting them to join her in a process of building knowledge, free of all emotion, in order to shed the best possible light on Nicolas Sarkozy. This call resulted in a collective work, *Petit précis de remise à niveau sur l'histoire africaine à l'usage du président Sarkozy*, the result of 25 contributions from African and European researchers. The chronological and thematic structuring of this book made it possible to challenge the stereotypes inherited from colonial ethnology that Nicolas Sarkozy conveyed, while delivering a history lesson with the aim of putting an end to the static vision of Africa.

---

[2] This expression comes from Adame Ba Konaré, in the general introduction she wrote for the book published in 2009, *Petit précis de remise à niveau sur l'histoire africaine à l'usage du président Sarkozy*.

So it was clear to us that this initiative, here as elsewhere in the world, had finally succeeded in persuading Africans, particularly those studying history at a university on the continent, about this issue. However, we were very surprised to discover that the theory relating to the supposed curse of the Black Man still persisted and remained difficult to grasp. This fact made our blood run cold. How can we still believe that in the 21st century, Africans can feel '' cursed ''?

To these students, to those who are destined to succeed us and to make Benin's education system more efficient and competitive at both continental and international level, we promised to compile all that is possible to know about the so-called curse of the Black Man, to present the intentions that led to the creation of this theory and to point out its shortcomings; shortcomings that clearly show that at no time has it constituted a historical or scientific reality. It was at this point that we decided to ensure that none of our students thought for a moment about their supposed curse because of the colour of their skin.

From that moment on, we approached the subject with a resolute determination, seeking to gather as many documents as possible in order to deepen our knowledge of the subject, on the one hand, and to provide clarification to our students, on the other.

From that moment on, we explored libraries and documentation centres in search of relevant information. We compiled significant documentation at the Benin National Library (Porto-Novo), the Zogbadjè Benin Excellence Library (Abomey-Calavi), the Library of the Benin Centre for Scientific Research and Innovation (Porto-Novo), the Benin National Archives (Porto-Novo), the Quai Branly Museum Media Library (Paris) and the Sorbonne Inter-University Library (Paris). In addition, we identified and exploited information on the Internet relating to the subject in question.

The subject matter is far removed from any form of stigmatisation of those who have long believed and tried to show that the Black Man is an abject being, devoid of any capacity for self-creation. Our intention is not to convince those who believe in the curse of the Black Man that Africa has a rich historical heritage that is crucial to building a present that offers hope and guarantees a better future for generations to come. No, that's not what we're about! We are fully aware that the African continent has travelled a road made up of successes and failures, glories and disillusions that must be taught with calmness and a certain objectivity.

In this essay, we are not seeking external approval to legitimize our existence and our history. Far be it from us to seek the liberation of the Black Man through Western intellectual recognition, sometimes tainted with racism. As the Nigerian writer Wole Soyinka said in 1962 at a writers' conference in Kampala, Uganda, in response to the movement that presented negritude as an emancipatory concept for Black People: '' A tiger does not proclaim its tigritude, it leaps ''. Given its past, Africa has nothing to prove to anyone. It is Africa and wishes to be recognised as such.

In this book, we do not seek to portray the African as an eternal victim, a being to whom everything has been denied and who, today, like a big child deprived of the real means to build himself up, is asking humanity to come to his aid. This is not the spirit that guides the writing of this book. Here, we are addressing our students, future colleagues representing the elite of Beninese society. We wish to provide them with a few tried and tested scientific elements concerning the non-malediction of Black People. Beyond our students, we wish to address Beninese in particular, and Africans in general, who wish to learn more about the subject. A scientific understanding of this subject will enable us to recognise the importance of the Black Man in the history of humanity.

In fact, those who try to defend this theory clearly show that they have a limited understanding of the history of the African continent and its peoples. This attitude is reminiscent of someone who, despite having a solid knowledge of a given subject, gives the impression of not having it. In any case, you will agree with us that it is very difficult to wake up someone who pretends to be asleep. It's hard to start a discussion with someone who thinks they know everything. You only have to look closely at the history of mankind to realise that, in the beginning, the Black Man felt no inferiority complex towards other communities.

Using his ingenuity, he succeeded in establishing societies that did not hesitate to welcome the most destitute. If we go back to the Bible, wasn't it to the Black Man, in Egypt, at the time of the Pharaohs, that Jacob, now Israel, and his descendants found refuge from the famine that was striking them? To make their journey easier, the pharaoh of the time provided them with carts, which were the most fashionable means of transport at the time[3]. A land of hospitality and Black People[4], ancient Egypt welcomed Abram, who later became Abraham, the father of Isaac and the grandfather of Jacob. He too, because of a famine in his country, decided to stay

---

[3] Read Genesis 46: 1-6.

[4] With regard to the African roots of the ancient Egyptians, it is advisable to consult Cheikh Anta Diop (1980, pp. 40-74) and Lilian Thuram (2014, p. 17-24) carefully.

with his wife in Egypt. The pharaoh of the time gave him sheep, goats, donkeys, she-asses, cattle, servants, maids and camels[5].

It is well known that, through the sciences, Egypt, the land of the Blacks, exerted an influence on the Greek mathematical tradition that was emerging between the 5th and 4th centuries BC. The story of Thales measuring the height of the pyramids is just one example of Greek intellectuals learning from the Egyptians; Herodotus and Plato described Egyptian methods of teaching and applying mathematics with admiration. It is therefore reasonable to assume that the fundamental foundations of the early mathematical efforts of the Greeks originated in ancient Egypt (A. Mehazzem, 2025, p. 11-23).

From the above, we can see that Africa, through Pharaonic Egypt, welcomed foreigners from the Hebrew world in search of social well-being and food, thanks to its abundant human labour force and rich agricultural and animal production[6]. Moreover, in the scientific sector, it had a significant impact on Europe thanks to the spread of mathematical

---

[5] Read Genesis 12: 10-20.

[6] During the reign of Ramses II, Egypt was '' the land of opulence and profusion, the land of full cooking pots that foreigners gazed upon with envy, the land of supply shops that Ramses had built everywhere, a country that was totally independent thanks to progressive agrarian techniques '' (P. Vandenberg, 1977, p. 127).

knowledge, which was improved and played a role in the fame of several non-African scientists. However, although this observation is indisputable, how can it be explained that for many people, despite their passion for sacred texts, the question of the alleged curse of the Black Man has been accepted? How can we understand that, despite the welcome given to Israel by one of the greatest ancient civilisations, which shared its roof and its grain with it, the supporters of the theory of the alleged curse of the Black Man, relying on sacred texts such as the Bible, have overlooked the fact that in chapter 22, verse 6 of the book of Numbers, it is specified that whoever curses the people of Israel will be cursed, while whoever blesses them will also be blessed? Could supporting a population in distress so generously on so many occasions lead Africa to a supposed perpetual curse, or to the continuation of a supposed curse, whatever the case may be?

The answers to the questions raised can be found in the three chapters of this book, which illustrate that, since time immemorial, the position of the African continent and Africans has never been peripheral in human society. On the contrary, Africa, often in the front line, has played a genuine part in the development of humanity in every conceivable aspect of life. The historical data we have chosen to cover in this book is not limited to Egypt alone. The greatness of this civilisation extended to the sub-Saharan region of the Dark Continent. It is here that we will extract numerous examples of Africa's contribution to the development of humanity.

The first chapter of the book explores in depth the myth linked to the supposed curse of Ham, and presents the elements that led Europe and the Arab-Muslim world to perceive Black People as inferior. The second chapter shows that the African continent is indisputably the original cradle of Man, regardless of skin colour. It also highlights the fact that the occupation of African territories by the representative of the genus Homo naturally led to the domestication and spread of plants essential for food. As for the final chapter of the study, it shows that medicine, mathematics and computer science were recognised scientific disciplines that were widely practised by Dark-Skinned individuals. These achievements have given them the opportunity to build societies free of any inferiority complex in relation to people of different skin tones.

CHAPTER 1

From the Ham myth to an examination of data on stereotypes associated with the hypothetical inferiority of black People

The first section of this chapter examines the myth associated with the so-called Curse of Ham. Is there really any indisputable historical evidence for this? Let's find out! The second part looks at the various factors that led Europe and the Arab-Muslim world to view Black People as inferior.

1.1. The myth of Ham or the alleged curse of the Black Man

In 1722, the Reverend Father Dom Augustin Calmet (1672-1757), a Benedictine monk and abbot of Saint Léopold of Nancy, published his *Diction-naire historique, critique, chronologique, géographi-*

que et littéral de la Bible, enriched with a large number of intaglio figures representing the Antiquities of Judaism. This work contains information about Ham. As the title of the work indicates, the information about one of Noah's sons was based mainly on Jewish and Christian sources, and was limited to the fact that Canaan, a son of Ham, had been subject to a "curse". The text emphasised this statement:

> Ham, the son of Noah and brother of Shem and Japheth (...) One day when Noah had drunk too much wine, Ham saw him lying in his tent and indecently uncovered himself. Instead of hiding it, he went and told Shem and Japheth. They covered themselves with a cloak and went back to throw the cloak over their father, thus covering his nakedness. When Noah woke up and heard what had happened, he said, *Let Canaan be cursed, and let him be a slave to his brothers.* These words suggest that Canaan had warned his father about Noah's nakedness. Others believe that Noah wanted to strike Ham in a more sensitive way, by giving his curse to Chanaan his son. Noah added: *Blessed be the Lord, the God of Shem: Let Ham be the slave of Shem: May God extend the possession of Japheth: Let Japheth dwell in the tents of Shem, and let Canaan be his slave* (A. Calmet, 1722, p. 194).

From this passage, it is easy to understand that beyond Canaan, Ham and all his descendants are condemned to be born into slavery as a result of the '' curse ''. It was not until the 1728 revised edition of Dom Augustin Calmet's dictionary that the '' Racial Blackening '' of Canaan's descendants, doomed to eternal servitude, became apparent, according to the French Benedictine. In this new edition of his work, Calmet draws on the research of the Arab historian Abū Jaʻfar Muhammad Ibn Jarīr Ibn Yazīd (839-923), more commonly known as Tabari. Taking up the writings of the author from what is now the Islamic Republic of Iran, Dom Augustin Calmet (quoted by B. Braude, 2002, p. 96) states:

> Ham. The author of the Tharik-Thabari teaches that Noah having given his curse to Ham and Chanaan, the effect of this curse was that not only were their posterity enslaved to their brothers, and born as it were in slavery, but also that suddenly the colour of their flesh became Black; for they hold that all Blacks come from Ham and Chanaan. When Noah saw this change so quickly, he was moved and prayed to God to inspire the masters of Chanaan to love him with tenderness and compassion. We can also see the effect of Noah's prayer in the servitude of the descendants of Ham, in that this type of Black Slave is cherished and sought after everywhere.

We wish to stress here that Dom Augustin Calmet was not the first European author to present the racial version of the '' curse '' of Ham. This function of legitimising the "curse", particularly in the seventeenth century, was highlighted by Oscar Bimwenyi-Kweshi (quoted by A. Quenum, 1993, p. 35), in his book on the *Discours théologique négro-africain. Problème des fondements*. In his analysis, he shows how the first missionaries in the French West Indies readily employed this theory. For example, a text from 1652 states: "That God has spread Europeans in America, to dwell in the homes of the Americans, descended from Shem; and that the descendants of Ham, who are our African negroes, will serve them there[7] ".

Moreover, Abū Jaʿfar Muhammad Ibn Jarīr Ibn Yazīd was not the first or only Arabic reference to support the racial version of the "curse" of Ham. Generally speaking, Mediterranean Arab literature from the eighth and ninth centuries onwards linked Black Skin colour[8] to negative personal traits, such as an

---

[7] See also David M. Whitford (2021).

[8] In attempting to define what is meant by "Black Skin ", dermatologist Antoine Mahé (2015, p. 2) points out that the word " Black " is inaccurate, because from a chromatic point of view, " Black Skin " is actually Brown. Biologically, this skin colour is due to melanin, a substance produced in greater quantities by the same number of melanocytes, which are nonetheless more active than those of " White Skin ". On observation of a histological section, without the use of specific stains, it is possible to see the pigmentation concentrated in the basal layer of the epidermis; on electron microscopy, the melanosomes appear larger, more nu-

unpleasant odour, repulsive appearance, disordered sexuality, and a certain savagery or deficiency. During this period, Arabo-Muslims not only regarded Black People as pagans, but increasingly as an inferior part of humanity doomed to enslavement, so much so that the Arabic term for a slave, *abid*, became virtually synonymous with Black (*zendj* being a more approximate term for "savages", notably used in Arabia). In this context, the enslavement of men with Black Skin was perceived as a normal situation, as was the use of pack animals (C. Coquery-Vidrovitch, 2021, p. 272-275; C. Coquery-Vidrovitch and É. Mesnard, 2019, p. 50; C. Coquery-Vidrovitch, 2016, p. 15-16; T. Diakité, 2008, p. 19).

It was by accurately adopting the Judeo-Christian[9] and Muslim versions of the "curse" of Ham that Cal-

---

merous and more diffusely distributed. Genetically, it is recognised that the level of skin pigmentation is determined by a small number of genes whose various alleles combine in different ways, giving rise to different skin tones. Although the expression '' Dark Skin '' may seem more precise, the imprecision of the usual term '' Black Skin '' is not too problematic once its limits are understood.

[9] According to Pierre Charles (1928, p. 723-724), certain rabbinical legends claim that Ham became completely Black as a result of his act of irreverence. As for the historian Agnès Lainé (1998), she indicates that the link between Black Populations and the descendants of Ham, who was cursed by his father for having glimpsed his nudity, dates back to the 6th century in Talmudic accounts and was transmitted through medieval tradition.

met's[10] Dictionary acquired the status of an essential reference work within the Christian World. For example, the eighteenth-century American theologian Jonathan Edwards (1703-1758), the son and grandson of pastors, recognised the importance of this work. This dictionary went through around thirty printings and editions, in at least four languages (English, French, Latin and Dutch); it was published in at least five countries on two continents over two centuries. Most versions cheerfully included the "curse" of Ham (B. Braude, 2002, p. 96-97).

The notion that Blacks are inferior to Whites, which would justify cursing Blacks, has even found its way into popular narratives widely disseminated in Africa, particularly within the sociolinguistic communities of the Ajatado cultural area. According to a story reported by Pierre-Claver Hujeson (1952, p. 39-41), it appears that God, *Mahu*, originally created Men equal, good and White. It is because of the reprehen-

---

[10] According to the writer André Wautier, Dom Augustin Calmet played a significant role in the spread of speculative Freemasonry. It is highly likely that he was a member of the secret Order of the Temple. *Dictionnaire des gnostiques et des principaux initiés*, p. 57. Cf. chrome-extension: // efaidnbmnnnibpcajpcglclefindmkaj / http://www.theologica.fr/!_Dictionnaires/Dictionnaires-%20 Encyclopedies.%20Ertc/Wautier%20Andr%C3%A9%20-%20 Dictionnaire%20des%20gnostiques%20et%20des%20principaux% 20initi%C3%A9s.pdf. Visited on 3 January 2026 at 11 hours 41 minutes.

sible actions of their ancestors that Africans have had their skin turned Black. What happened to give them this skin colour?

To this question, the author replies that it was man himself who altered God's creation. Some, satisfied with their lot, worked and fed themselves abundantly. Others, dissatisfied, allowed themselves to become lazy and ran out of food. The lazy ones then began to oppress the workers, who had to appeal to *Mahu*. *Mahu* appeared before an assembly made up of workers and lazy people and said: "There are men who complain, who murmur and who only want disorder. Today I'm proposing a way for you to realise that it's greed that gives rise to all your misfortunes".

In front of the huge assembly, the servants of God, according to the story, placed three prepared bags, sealed and filled with unknown objects. '' Dissatisfied, exclaimed *Mahu*, choose leaders from among yourselves and let them take the bag that suits them ''. Immediately, several leaders of the sloths came forward and examined the three bags from every angle and, after discussion, took the heaviest bag. As for the leaders of the workers, they chose the lightest of the two remaining bags. Following these events, *Mahu* declared:

> You have, in the bag you have freely chosen, the tools of your happiness. Your Creator and Master won't change a thing. All that remains is for you to separate, to move away and forget your old arguments. There are two regions, the North where it's cold and the South where it's hot. Let the group that has chosen the heavier bag take one direction, and the other group go in the opposite direction.

After a month's march, the workers and the lazy settled in the country where they had arrived. The workers had travelled twice as far to get as far away as possible from their belligerent brothers. Once settled, the two groups opened their bags. In the sloths' bag were a hoe, an axe, an adze, a dugout cutter, a sickle for cutting grass for roofing, a cutter, a trowel for building earthen walls, a calabash, cowries and many other things. In the workers' bags were finer work tools, gold, silver, silk cloth, written and unwritten paper, quill pens, ink, etc. The popular story also points out that the workers became the ancestors of the Whites, still called *Yovo* in *fongbé*, while the quarrelsome descended from the Blacks. The Blacks, who are generally unclothed, became Black because of the sun. The Whites became Black because they were always clothed. At the end of the story, the reader is reminded that: "Whites and Blacks have freely chosen their destiny; it will not change. Blacks will never become Whites" or "Blacks can always take advantage of Whites. By imitating Whites, we can improve our lot, which has been spoiled by greed".

Faced with all these theories put forward by authors from Jewish, Christian and Muslim backgrounds, who consider the Black Man to be a being cursed by the Creator, are we really in a position to affirm that they are based on the Bible? What is the position of the Old Testament regarding the hypothetical story of the '' curse '' of the Black Man by Noah, a servant of God? In order to provide some answers to the question raised here, we will look at two biblical characters, namely Ham and Canaan. Who is Ham? He was one of Noah's three sons, born after 2470 BC (Genesis 5: 32; 7: 6; 11: 10). He may have been the youngest (Genesis 9: 24), but he is mentioned second in Genesis 5: 32, Genesis 6: 10 and elsewhere. In Genesis 10: 21, Shem is referred to as '' the brother of the elder Japheth ''. Ham fathered four sons: Kush, Mizraim, Put and Canaan (Genesis 10: 6; 1 Chronicles 1: 8). These sons are the ancestors of the Ethiopians, Egyptians, various Arab and African tribes and the Canaanites.

It is argued that some of the Chamitic peoples mentioned in Genesis chapter 10 used a Semitic language. However, this does not call into question the fact that they were of Chamitic origin or that they originally spoke a Chamitic language. Indeed, many groups adopted the language of their conquerors, that of other peoples with whom they interacted or that of the country in which they had settled. Some time later, Ham was involved in an incident that resulted in a curse for his son Canaan. Noah, having drunk too much wine, was uncovered in his tent. Ham saw his father's nakedness, but instead of showing the respect a son owes to Noah, the patriarch, servant and prophet chosen by God to preserve mankind, Ham told his two brothers what he had seen. Shem and Japheth, for their part, showed proper respect for their father by going backwards with a cloak to cover him, so as not to disgrace his nakedness. When Noah woke up, he heard what had happened and cursed not Ham, but Canaan, the son of Ham. In his subsequent blessing to Shem, which also included a blessing for Japheth, he ignored Ham and only mentioned Canaan, cursing him and prophesying that he would become the slave of Shem and Japheth (Genesis 9: 20-27).

It is possible that Canaan was directly involved in the incident without his father correcting him. Alternatively, Noah, in speaking, could have perceived in advance that Canaan's descendants would inherit Ham's evil tendency, perhaps already evident in his son Canaan. The curse was partially fulfilled when the Israelites, descendants of the Semites, subdued the Canaanites. Those who survived (like the Gibeonites - Joshua 9) became Israel's slaves[11]. Centuries later, the curse continued to be fulfilled when the descendants of Canaan were enslaved by the Japhaic world powers of the Medo-Persian Empire, Greece and Rome (Watch Tower Bible and Tract Society, vol. 1, 1997, p. 482).

One question may be asked to clarify the reader's knowledge: where are the territories inhabited by the descendants of Shem, Japheth and their nephew Canaan? Let's start with Canaan. He was the ancestor of 11 tribes who eventually settled in the region along the eastern Mediterranean, between Egypt and Syria (Genesis 10: 15-19; 1 Chronicles 16: 18).

Japheth is recognised as the ancestor of the Indo-European branch of humanity. The names of his sons and grandsons appear in ancient writings relating to peoples who lived mainly in the northern and western parts of the Fertile Crescent. They spread from the Caucasus eastwards into Central Asia, but also westwards through Asia Minor, reaching the islands and coasts of Europe as far as Spain. Some Arabic traditions claim that one of Japheth's sons was also the ancestor of the Chinese people (Watch

---

[11] See also Tidiane N'Diaye (2008, p. 56).

Tower Bible and Tract Society, vol. 1, 1997, p. 1236-1237).

Shem is recognised as the ancestor of the Semitic peoples: the Elamites, the Assyrians, the first Chaldeans, the Hebrews, the Arameans, several Arab tribes and possibly the Lydians of Asia Minor. This would suggest that the population of Shem was concentrated mainly in south-west Asia, encompassing most of the Fertile Crescent and occupying a considerable part of the Arabian Peninsula (Watch Tower Bible and Tract Society, vol. 2, 1997, p. 923).

According to the information provided above, considering the geographical space occupied by the descendants of Canaan, it can be said that several authors have wrongly maintained that the Blackness and slavery of the members of this human community resulted from the '' curse '' pronounced on Canaan. In reality, as can be seen, Canaan's descendants are not essentially '' dark '' in complexion. Rather, the Blacks come from Kush and perhaps Put, who were also sons of Ham and were not involved in the incident or affected by the curse. Indeed, the available evidence shows a connection between Put and the Libyans of the North African region. The term Put is sometimes translated as '' Libyans '' or '' Libya '' (Watch Tower Bible and Tract Society, vol. 2, 1997, p. 630). Although descendants of Kush have been identified in Arabia, in the majority of cases the ancestor's name clearly refers to a region in Africa and, where the link is clear, translators simply translate Kush as Ethiopia. Kush is systematically associated with Egypt (Isaiah 20: 3-5; 43: 3; Jeremiah 46: 7-9) and Libya (2 Chronicles 12: 2; Daniel 11: 43; Nahum 3: 9[12]).

From what has just been said, it is possible to conclude that an objective and meticulous approach to the Bible does not make it possible to establish a link between Dark-Skinned people and the curse of Canaan. Nevertheless, as we write these words, stereotypes remain, perpetuating the idea that we are inferior to others; these tenacious prejudices persist despite the concrete evidence showing that Black People are not affected by the curse pronounced by Noah on one of his grandsons.

Some people attribute the '' curse '' of the Black People to their history of slavery, which goes back to very ancient times. We respond to these people without hesitation by affirming that Man has always been subject to the power of others. Indeed, slavery has never been a phenomenon exclusive to Africans.

---

[12] For further information on the relationship between the descendants of Kush and Africa, it is advisable to consult Werner Vycichl (1957, p. 177-179), Cheikh Anta Diop (1979), François de Medeiros (1985, p. 128-132) and Tidiane N'Diaye (2008, p. 48-56).

For example, among the Ancient Greeks, it was considered particularly shameful not to have slaves in one's service. In Athens, four centuries before the Christian era, there were at least 250,000 slaves. Most of the slaves, mainly Blacks, came from Upper Egypt, where the Nubians were particularly valued. Slavery was also widespread among the Romans. In the course of their many campaigns of conquest, they enslaved large numbers of captives whom they had defeated or taken from their colonies. Most of these captives were White. It is now recognised that Roman Antiquity marked the beginning of large-scale slavery for the production of goods. At that time, up to 3,000,000 slaves lived in Italy, representing around 30% of the population (T. N'Diaye, 2008, p. 13-18).

The practice of slavery was widespread among the Jews long before the Christian era. Within this community, wars, poverty and crime were the main causes that led men into slavery. Prisoners of war often became slaves to those who had captured them, or were sold into slavery (2 Kings 5: 2; Watch Tower Bible and Tract Society, vol. 1, 1997, p. 793). In Israelite society, an individual who fell into poverty could choose to sell himself or his children into slavery to pay off his debts (Exodus 21: 7; Leviticus 25: 39, 47; 2 Kings 4: 1). A thief who was unable to repay the amount stolen was sold to cover what he had stolen and, it seems, regained his freedom once all charges against him had been dropped (Exodus 22: 2-4).

Among the Israelites, the status of a Hebrew slave differed from that of a foreign slave, whether resident or immigrant. While a non-Hebrew slave remained the property of his master and could be inherited from generation to generation (Leviticus 25: 44-46), a Hebrew slave had to be freed either at the end of his seventh year of slavery or in the year of Jubilee, whichever came first. During the period of slavery, the Hebrew slave was to be treated as an employee (Exodus 21: 2; Leviticus 25: 10; Deuteronomy 15: 2).

Specific rules applied to a Hebrew woman who became a slave. Her master could take her as a concubine or give her in marriage to his son. In the latter case, she was treated in accordance with the law for daughters. Even if the son married another woman, there was to be no reduction in his food, clothing or conjugal rights. If the son neglected this obligation, the wife could regain her freedom without having to pay a redemption price (Exodus 21: 7-11).

The muslim world also experienced and practised slavery. The Persian historian, geographer and poet Ahmed ben Mohammed Ibn al-Faqih al-Hamadânî (quoted by T. N'Diaye, 2008, p. 188-189), who lived in the tenth century AD, considered that the enslavement of individuals from non-Muslim communities was perfectly normal and natural: '' From the western sea, male slaves, Romans, Franks, Lombards and Roman and Andalusian women arrived in the East ''. Another Arab scholar, Ibn Haukal (1122-1213), author of treatises on physics, medicine and grammar in the 12th century, added: '' The most beautiful article imported from Spain are the slaves, girls and handsome boys who were taken from the land of the Franks and from Galicia. All the Slav eunuchs to be found on earth are brought from Spain and as soon as they arrive, they are castrated '' (T. N'Diaye, 2008, p. 189).

Three factors put an end to the supply of European slave labour to the Arab-Muslim world. Firstly, Russia, by subduing the Tatars and taking control of Crimea, prevented this activity from continuing; secondly, Europeans, by colonising the Muslim world, actively opposed the enslavement of their fellow human beings; and thirdly, Turkey, under European pressure, stopped supplying the Arab world with White Slaves. However, the '' White deficit '' was largely offset by an increased supply of slaves from the African continent. For centuries, a vast extraction of men and children destined to become eunuchs was carried out in most African countries. On their arrival in the Arab-Muslim world, many African slaves were assigned to guard harems. However, most of them were assigned domestic work or joined the armed forces. Other uncastrated adult males were exploited in salt and gold mines, and even on farms. After the Europeans, Black Africans were sold on the markets of Baghdad, Yemen and Egypt (T. N'Diaye, 2008, p. 189-190).

In the context of slavery in Arab-Muslim regions, Brown Women were the most valuable. Nubian and Abyssinian women were particularly prized. They were often used for sexual slavery. They were also used as ladies-in-waiting and were renowned for their domestic skills. In general, all these women were reduced to a state of dependence and absolute submission to their master (T. N'Diaye, 2008, p. 161-162).

It is now indisputable that slavery is in no way specific to Africa. Moreover, it has been clearly shown that the African is not the one who was struck by a curse by Noah. So why do some people continue to see Black People as inferior? This question, which may seem simple but is full of depth and truth, finds its answer in the assertion that this phenomenon stems from human nature, which is often inclined to value itself by projecting onto others the worst defects. On what credible basis can the Brown Man still be considered an inferior being? None, except that as long as they convince themselves that the other is insufficiently "civilised", this could legitimise their way of life, which they strive to impose on the rest of the world.

In the rest of the essay, we examine various factors that have led Europe and the Arab-Muslim world to perceive the Brown as inferior. The intention here is not simply to list them, but to challenge them by confronting them with arguments that are both scientific and understandable.

1.2 Seeking information on the prejudices associated with the alleged inferiority of Black People

Studies by Tidiane N'Diaye (2008, p. 48-49) emphasise that the mass importation of Brown Slaves profoundly affected Arab-Muslim perceptions of Africans. For them, it was when sub-Saharan Africa became the main source of slaves for the Slave Trade that Black People began to be associated with servitude, and their skin colour with a rejection of Islam. Among the thinkers who developed racial ideologies about Africans was Ibn Khaldun (2006, p. 170, 213), who was born in 1332 and died in 1406[13]. In his

---

[13] According to Daniel Amara Cissé (1988, p. 45), Ibn Khaldun, originally from Tunis, successively held the positions of secretary, head of the chancellery, minister in charge of recruiting mercenar-

work entitled *"Les Prolégomènes"*, he argued that Black People were "more like wild animals than reasonable beings". The author even argued that Blacks were generally defined by their lightness, inconstancy and emotionalism, and that they felt an irrepressible urge to dance whenever they heard music. As a result, they were considered to have little intelligence. For Ibn Khaldun, the joy and happiness of the Blacks were essentially animal spirits.

In the fourteenth century, when this Arab-Berber author was expressing these ideas, he was simply unaware that the '' joy and gaiety '' displayed by dark-haired people had therapeutic properties. Indeed, according to Alexia Cheval (2022, p. 7), the laughter and good humour encapsulated in the terms '' joy '' and '' cheerfulness '' encourage creativity and efficiency in an active individual, boost self-confidence, and engender a dynamic and willing state of mind. Ibn Khaldun (2006, p. 210) was unaware of these beneficial elements for the human being, because he had simply engaged in a random and biased demonstration which maintained that Black People lived in regions where heat prevailed over their temperament,

---

ies, prisoner, ambassador and writer, among others. He travelled through various parts of North Africa, from Tunis to Fez and from Bougie to Tlemcen, as well as Cairo; he also spent time in Seville and Granada.

which would explain their alleged stupidity and degree of inferiority.

In his desire to prove that the Browns were inferior to the Arab-Muslims, Ibn Khaldun (2006, p. 170, 213) did not hesitate to declare that they practised anthropophagi and liked to "indulge in dancing whenever they found the slightest opportunity; so that everywhere they have a reputation for madness". What he didn't know at the time, however, was that dancing is beneficial to human health. In fact, a study carried out over a decade ago by Sylvie Fortin, Sylvie Trudelle and Geneviève Rail (2008, p. 17) on a sample of 20 professional dancers from the Montreal area, including 15 women and 5 men, with an average age of 33.9 years for the women and 37.3 years for the men, revealed that dance maintains an intimate relationship with physical and psychological health. For the researchers, physical health is a key element in the development of the functional dimension of health. However, this is part of a global approach to health, which links the various aspects of the individual, including the psychological dimension. The expressions "overall state of balance", "well-being" and "happiness" appear frequently in the dancers' discourse (more so than among the dancers) when they try to define what health means. For them, this highlights a significant interconnection between psychological health and bodily functionality. They also emphasised the importance of cultivating "inner strength" and "self-confidence", seen as "an extra muscle to develop", qualities which, to a large extent, guarantee a healthy attitude towards themselves and their often demanding profession.

In his work *Les Prolégomènes*, Ibn Khaldoun (2006, p. 212-213) also set out to identify the characteristics of Ham's progeny. For him, it is indisputable that the genealogists of his time, as well as those of earlier periods, "regarded all the Black-Skinned inhabitants of the south as the descendants of Ham; and, not knowing how to explain the colour of these peoples, they set about propagating a tradition that does not stand up to scrutiny". As explained in the previous chapter, it is wrong to assert that all the descendants of Ham are Dark-Skinned: only those from Kush and Put can legitimately claim descent. At this point, Ibn Khaldun's argument for the inferiority of Black-Skinned Man is not based on reliable scientific evidence.

Using dance, joy and gaiety to legitimise the supposed inferiority of one human community over another is, in truth, mind-boggling. To do so is tantamount, for example, to asserting that Danxomè (improperly referred to as Dahomey), which came into being in the first half of the 17th century, had the attributes of a city inhabited by men and women who were considered to be "uncivilised" or "inferior". Indeed, research into this entity has shown that it particularly valued music and dance (M. Quenum, 1935; da Cruz, 1954; B. Koudjo, 1988; B. Koudjo, 2005; D. M. Houénoudé, 2009; Th. Gléssougbé, 2012; S. Soloum and A. G. Gomina, 2022; M. Vido and A. Vido, 2022).This is despite being recognised by both African and Western researchers as one of the most structured African monarchies from a political, economic, socio-cultural and religious point of view, etc. (A. A. Vido, Y. S. Yoboué and T. Azonhè, 2024). Following the criteria established by Ibn Khaldun, should we consider the Kingdom founded by the *Agasuvi* as one of the most absurd human organisations? Absolutely not!

It is acknowledged that the accession of Louis XVI to the throne in 1775, and the arrival of Marie Antoinette in France, enabled music to develop at Versailles, which thus acquired a much more important role within royalty. This transformation is observable because the end of Louis XV's reign was accompanied by the end of an era in which music had lost its visibility at Versailles. During his last years on the throne, Louis XV rarely stayed at the château, preferring Fontainebleau instead. With the royal residence half-empty, music occupied a marginal place (R. Maireau, N. Boucetta and B. Langlois, 2017, p. 4).

In a Master's thesis devoted to the modern period, François Caussin (2016) sought to explore the musical dimensions of various social and public practices in Grenoble, as well as the search for musical traces in the homes of private individuals, particularly among the local aristocracy, before these enthusiasts came together within the *Académie du Concert* from 1724 onwards. To carry out his study, the author focused on a specific social group: professionals in the musical professions, such as organists or masters of music and psalters working for the Church, as well as the city's independent musicians, notably instrumentalists, dancing masters and artisanal instrumentalists. This study examines in detail the members of the Farinel family, and in particular the life of Michel Farinel, a musician from Grenoble and Europe.

In the light of the data presented above, on the one hand, and of the ideology supported by Ibn Khaldun, which evokes the alleged inferiority of a human community through its close links with dance and music, on the other, we might consider that French society in the modern era was considered to be '' uncivilised '' or '' savage ''. In reality, adopting such a shortcut in the analysis of historical events is very risky and calls into question the assertions of the Arab-Berber author. The arguments put forward by Ibn Khaldun are clearly obsolete and have difficulty convincing minds marked by rigour and objectivity in their scientific production.

Although it has now been established that Ibn Khaldun's erroneous ideas were largely supported by authors who preceded or followed him in their mission, it is undeniable that during the pre-Islamic period, Browns and Arabs coexisted without prejudice. According to the research of Tidiane N'Diaye (2008, p. 43), the first conflicts did not take place until the beginning of the 6th century AD. By 702, the Ethiopians had laid siege to the entire Arabian coast and the port of Jeddah. Their forces had twice tried in vain to invade part of Arabia. In a final major offensive, the Ethiopians were defeated by the Persians, leaving many prisoners to be enslaved. As allies of the Byzantines, these Ethiopians had played a very active role in Arabia. The Arabs and Persians therefore had a knowledge of the Black peoples through these few battles.

In those days, Arabs did not express contempt or rejection of Africans. On the contrary, Africans were honoured and many of the companions of the Prophet Mohamed (570-632) were of mixed descent with an Ethiopian grandmother. Although the majority of Ethiopians remained faithful to orthodox Christianity, they were nevertheless respected by the Arabs, even after the first Islamic expansion. Moreover, during the Prophet Mohamed's lifetime, in 615, several of his disciples from Mecca, fleeing persecution by the Khoraishite dynasty, were welcomed and protected by the Ethiopians in Aksum. To these refugees, the prophet had declared: "If you go to Africa, you will find a king under whom no one is persecuted. It is a land of justice where God will bring rest from your tribulations". On another occasion, he is said to have added: "Avoid any quarrel with the Ethiopians, for they have shared nine-tenths of the courage of mankind".

Moreover, when Bilal Ibn Rabah, a slave of Ethiopian origin freed by Abu Bakr, the Prophet's brother-in-law, embraced Islam, Mohamed appointed him as the first muezzin in history, meaning the person responsible for calling for prayer from the top of the mosque's minaret. According to Khalid Mohammad Khalid (2010, p. 48), Bilal Ibn Rabah did not seem to attach much importance to the praise he received. He often lowered his gaze to express his humility: "I am more of an Abyssinian... I was a slave...". The Prophet Mohamed had as his follower in Islam his freed slave and adopted son, Zayd Ibn Haritha, who was: "small in stature, very dark, with a somewhat squashed nose[14]" (K. M. Khalid, 2010, p. 135). The

---

[14] It is essential to note that in the Arab-Muslim imagination, certain criteria were recognised as indicators of the curse linked to the African. These criteria included Dark Skin colour, curly hair,

achievements of many Brown Arabs, both freed and of mixed race, have long been celebrated through tales and legends. Among them stands out Antara, an eminent warrior and poet whose father belonged to the Arab tribe of the 'Abs, while his mother, Zabiba, was an Ethiopian slave. Antara even became an icon of Arab heroism in a chivalric novel, taking part in wars against Persia, Byzantium and the Crusaders (P. K. Gnagny, 2023, p. 163-174).

In reality, the underestimation of the Dark-Skinned Man that developed in the Arab-Muslim world represented a simple yet effective method designed to systematically deny dignity to those it sought to en-

---

fine eyebrows, a flat nose, thick lips, good teeth, unpleasant body odour, cracks in the skin of the feet and hands, and a large, virile limb (M. Cissoko, 2019, p. 42). If we examine these criteria, we realise that none of them is based on solid scientific foundations. Instead, we are confronted with simplistic stereotypes that reveal the low level of analysis of their authors. Who can seriously consider bad body odour as a sign of a curse ? And even if this is accepted, who can claim that Africans did not care about their body odour ? In reporting on the use of baths in what is now known as southern Benin, the Frenchmen L. Brunet and Louis Giethlen (1900, p. 268, 270) did not hesitate to mention that at the end of the nineteenth century : '' Bathing is a general practice on the Slave Coast ; men and women wash frequently in plenty of water, even several times a day. Cleanliness and hygiene make it their duty to do so, as the almost constant perspiration they undergo means they are very susceptible to skin diseases (...) It is after bathing that the Negresses smear themselves with oil, ointments and cosmetics ''.

slave. This radical transformation coincided with the beginning of the great Arab conquests and the subjugation of defeated or Islamised peoples. At the same time, scholars tried to paint the image of enslaved Africans in Black, constructing increasingly fanciful theories, even though none of them visited Black Africa before the 14th century. Their very limited knowledge of the subject only allowed them to relay legends and other prejudices about Africans[15]. The Arab-Muslim attitude resulted in a total cost of more than 17,000,000 captives taken from sub-Saharan

---

[15] Let's face it, not all Arab writers supported Ibn Khaldun's ideology. In the eighth and nineteenth centuries, several authors committed themselves to defending Black People against this social violence and prejudice. Among those who tackled this subject, Al-Jahiz (776-867) stands out with his epistle, which is the first work in this field. Abu al-"abbas al-nashi" also wrote an epistle entitled 'tafdil al-Sud ala al-bid', meaning '' The superiority of Blacks over Whites ''. Muhammad ibn Khalaf al-mirzban also produced an epistle entitled '' al-Sudan wa fadluhum ala al-bidan '', meaning '' Blacks and their superiority over Whites ''. For his part, Abu al-Faraj al-Jawziy wrote an epistle entitled '' tanwir al-ghibsh fi fadl al-Sudan wa al-habash '', which can be translated as '' illuminating the twilight on the preference of Blacks and Ethiopians ''. Al-Jahiz, a pioneer and emblematic figure in this field, had Black ancestors, although he often adopted a neutral stance in the face of Black criticism. It is crucial to note that the writings of these defenders of the Black cause were above all poetic and rhetorical. They endeavoured to represent the opposing camp in order to promote literary eloquence and show the excellence of the self by highlighting the beauty of what is often perceived by one's opposite in society (M. Cissoko, 2019, p. 42-43).

Africa between the seventh and early twentieth centuries. It is particularly difficult not to describe this trade as genocide of the Brown Peoples, due to the massacres, cruel raid and mass castration (M-A. Pérouse de Montclos, 2002, p. 751-759; T. N'Diaye, 2008, p. 48, 221; M. Cissoko, 2019, p. 38-45).

In Europe before the 18th century, the Africans present were not exclusively confined to servile status. Although a significant proportion were, thousands of others enjoyed full European citizenship and belonged to various levels of society: servants, mistresses, writers, engineers, sailors, soldiers, officers, generals, philosophers, workers, musicians, wealthy landowners, dukes, princes, saints, clerics, sportsmen, painters and so on. At the time, the fact that some Africans had been reduced to slavery in Europe was not in itself evidence of inferiority, since there were also Europeans, both Brown and White, who shared this servile condition (D. Gnammankou, 2008, p. 64; V. Callot, 2023, p. 175-177).

Indeed, according to research by Hayri Gökşin Özkoray (2017, p. 229-231), as early as the Middle Ages, among the Abbasids, and later in Mamluk Egypt, the term mamlūk referred to slaves with White Skin (mainly of Caucasian origin), while the word abid referred to Black Slaves from sub-Saharan Africa. At that time, the Genoese authorities had obtained permission from the Mongol Khan to establish a trading post in Caffa in 1266. From this fortified town in Gazaria in the Crimea, Genoese merchants managed the transit of slaves of Circassian, Russian, Abkhazian, Mingrelian, Laz, Tatar, Iranian and Polish origin towards the south and west.

Azov, the other key port for Pontic trade, had been colonised by Venice in 1333. For the Serenissima, Azov was an answer to the growing need for slaves for its colony on Crete. Between 1351 and 1353, the two Italian cities were at odds over dominance of the Black Sea trade, which was rich in furs, silk, spices, precious stones and slaves. Rivalry between the Venetians and Genoese hampered the ability of either city to control the Pontic Slave Trade, where Italian merchants acquired individuals already enslaved in inland regions stretching as far as the Caspian Sea and sometimes as far as Central Asia. In 1459, the Senate of Venice expressed its concern at the scarcity of human labour; the Genoese, more daring, turned more towards the Muslim territories of Spain and North Africa to obtain slaves, which they transported to Seville and the Canary Islands.

Ottoman expansion north of the Black Sea had a significant impact on the supply of White Slaves from Mamluk Egypt, while at the same time considerably reducing the number of Tatar, Russian, Turkish and Circassian or Adyghe Slaves in Italian cities. This change marked the shift in the activities of Genoese and Venetian traders in the international Slave Trade from the Black Sea to the western Mediterranean and the Atlantic Ocean at the end of the fifteenth century. Following the determined opposition of central and western Europeans to Ottoman military expansion from the mid-sixteenth century onwards, the Crimean Tatars became the main suppliers of slaves to the major Ottoman cities: their attacks targeting Poland, Lithuania, Russia and the Caucasus became more frequent between 1514 and 1654.

As we have seen from a few examples, until the seventeenth century, Whites were subjected to the condition of servitude by other Whites as well as by Arabs. During this period, the Darker-Skinned Slave was certainly not the only one to be perceived as a "savage", a "barbarian" or a "chattel". The innovative element that began to emerge timidly in the 17th century, and became omnipresent in the 18th and 19th centuries, was that the entire slave population in the American colonies and the West Indies was Black. At the same time, slave owners were White. In order to justify the institution of slavery and maintain "racial purity", pseudo-scientific theories about the inherent intellectual inferiority of Black People were widely propagated on the European and American continents (D. Gnammankou, 2008, p. 64; V. Callot, 2023, p. 177-180).

It was in the wake of the enlightenment and rationalism that European scholars and thinkers began to organise the different human varieties into categories, in the same way that plants and animals had been classified. They had heated debates about the origins of humanity: the main debate was between monogenists[16], such as the German philosophers Emmanuel Kant (1724-1804) and Johann Gottfried Von Herder (1744-1803), and polygenists[17], such as the French writer and philosopher François Marie Arouet, better known as Voltaire (1694-1778), on this issue; it is important to remember that, theoretically, Christianity is monogenist. Added to this is the idea of determinism, which supports the link between soil, climate, food and human anatomy, as well as morals and society; then the evolutionary theories of the english naturalist Charles Robert Darwin (1809-1882) come into play. Although he was a monogenist, his theory of natural selection led him to believe that some "races" were "less evolved" than others. The English philosopher Herbert Spencer (1820-1903) seized on the idea of evolution and

---

[16] Monogenism or monocentrism is the ancient theory that all men and women derive from a single type, population or even couple.

[17] Polygenism was a theory that claimed that humanity was in fact divided into species or races of different origins. It was opposed to monogenism.

applied it to society, asserting the progressive victory of the " fittest " as the law of history.

From then on, there was a fear that races considered inferior would prevail over those considered superior, a fear that their blood could be contaminated and that racial degeneration would occur. It was the Frenchman, Count Arthur de Gobineau (1816-1882), who first proposed a theory on the hierarchy of races - he did not linger over a definition of race, which he took for granted - and supported the myth of distinct blood. On the one hand, he classifies the races: White, intelligent; Black, sensitive and bestial; Yellow, industrial. Naturally, the superior race is White, which is divided into Caucasians (Germanic and Frankish Aryans, Celts and Slavs) and Semites. He also defended the idea of biological determinism and associated the biological with the social. According to him, the law of the history of civilisations states that the White race must die, because its blood will inevitably be contaminated by that of others. In reality, he applied a totally aristocratic and biologically determined vision of noble heredity to human history[18].

---

[18] One of the aims of Gobineau's research was to exclude Black-Skinned populations from Noah's descendants and to clarify the origins of the Egyptians during the Pharaonic era (A. Lainé, 1998). Apart from Gobineau, it is possible to mention the French anatomist Georges Cuvier (1769-1832), who was an ardent de-

Initially, Gobineau's lamentations had no impact. He did, however, enjoy a significant following, particularly in Germany, thanks to the naturalised British-German essayist Houston Stewart Chamberlain (1855-1927), who had a major influence on German thought from the reign of Wilhelm II to that of Adolf Hitler. Gobineau marked the transition from racial to racist thinking. Science became involved, through anthropology, anthropometry, phrenology and craniology, among others. This shift was to encourage the scientistic theorisation of what would come to be known as '' racism '', and which would invade history, anthropology and politics. Fear and hatred of others were transformed into a tool of government and exploitation that would be used in un-

---

fender of comparative anatomy and paleontology. This zoologist was interested not only in contemporary species, but also in extinct animals. Man, as an animal species, was one of his subjects of study. Georges Cuvier was part of the scientific movement of the early twentieth century, an era accompanied by his ideological prejudices. He conducted research on sub-Saharan Africans, whom he considered '' the most degraded of all human races, whose forms come closest to being brutal ''. Shortly after the death of Saartjie Baartman, nicknamed '' The Hottentot Venus '', he undertook to dissect it in the name of '' scientific progress ''. He made a complete mold of his body and removed its skeleton, brain, and genitals, which were kept in jars of formalin. In 1817, he presented the results of his work and studies before the Academy of Medicine. The dissemination of his research illustrates well the racist positions that characterized Western science in the 19th century (G. Boëtsch, 2011, p. 64).

imaginable ways (A. Lainé, 1998; N. Savy, 2015, p. 36; FME, 2023).

Following the example of the Arab-Muslims, the Europeans implemented a policy aimed at justifying, without any convincing scientific evidence, the enslavement of a human community, the Black People. Based on a totally erroneous interpretation of the Bible and on pseudo-scientific theories, they succeeded in presenting Black Man as an inferior being, devoid of soul, history and intellect capable of self-determination and organisation in all areas of life. Convinced of this untruth, which relieved them of their conscience, the Whites played a large part in the deportation of millions of Africans as slaves to Europe, America and the West Indies.

According to the British historian Anne Ruderman (2022, p. 94), the Transatlantic Slave Trade spanned four centuries, beginning with the first Portuguese ships carrying captives to Lisbon and ending with the last slave ship leaving Cadiz for Cuba on 26 October 1864. During this period, some 12.5 million Africans were torn from their lands and chained in steerage, while 10.6 million managed to survive the terrible conditions of the crossing[19]. For the author,

---

[19] These figures are shared by Catherine Coquery-Vidrovitch and Éric Mesnard (2019, p. 124) who write : '' In total, at least 12.5 million men and women were taken on board the slave ships. 1.8

although these figures are shocking, they underestimate the true scale of the human tragedy. In fact, in addition to the 12.5 million captives taken on board the ships, between 2 and 5 million victims perished during their forced march from the interior to the sea or in the squalid shelters where they were confined while awaiting embarkation. The majority of those who survived the crossing were forced to work as convicts in the sugar cane fields and sugar mills of the West Indies, where almost 10% of captives died within a year of disembarkation. For European slavers, this high mortality rate meant that the pace of the trade had to be stepped up and more and more men had to be transported to the plantations in the New World. For the captives from the African continent, this mortality rate was a quantitative indicator of the brutality of their existence.

The theories developed to establish the superiority of Whites over Blacks would foster ideas in the minds of Whites that would lead to the colonisation of the African continent from the 19th century onwards. The notion of the West's '' civilising mission '' was put forward by the French writer Victor Hugo (1802-1885), who gave a speech on 18 May 1879 at a banquet celebrating the abolition of slavery, in

---

million of them perished during the crossing ''. See also Catherine Coquery-Vidrovitch (2016, p. 128-129).

which he saw Africa as an unknown and barbaric universe to which Europe, in order to become a new world, had to bring civilisation:

> What a land Africa is! Asia has its history, America has its history, Australia itself has its history; Africa has no history. A sort of vast and obscure legend envelops it. Rome touched it in order to eradicate it; and when it thought it had been delivered from Africa, Rome cast upon this immense dead woman one of those epithets that cannot be translated: Africa portentosa! (Applause). This is more and less than a prodigy. It is the absolute horror. The tropical blaze is indeed Africa. It seems that to see Africa is to be blinded. Too much sun is too much night. Well, this fear will disappear. The two colonising peoples, two great free peoples, France and England, have already seized Africa; France holds it from the west and from the north; England holds it from the east and from the south. Italy is now accepting its share of this colossal task. America is joining our efforts, for the unity of peoples is revealed in everything. Africa is important to the world[20].

---

[20] Http :chrome-extension://efaidnbmnnnibpcajpcglclefindmkaj /https://ecole-lacanienne.net/wp-content/uploads/2016   /04/2-23-janvier-2016-Texte-de-Victor-Hugo-.pdf. Visited on 8 January 2026 at 15 hours 21 minutes.

The same goes for the French statesman Jules Ferry (1832-1893) who, in his speech to the Chamber of Deputies on 28 July 1885, declared: ''It must be openly stated that indeed the superior races have a right vis-à-vis the inferior races ... I repeat that there is a right for the superior races, because there is a duty for them. They have the duty to civilize the inferior races[21]... ''. These declarations will lead to the holding of the Berlin Conference (15 November 1884-26 February 1885), which will mark the organization and European cooperation for the sharing and division of Africa[22]. This conference will lead to

---

[21] Http : chrome-extension://efaidnbmnnnibpcajpcglclefindmkaj /https://lvhpog.e-monsite.com/medias/files/1885-discours-colonial-de-jules-ferry.docx.pdf. Visited on 8 January 2026 at 15 hours 24 minutes.

[22] One of the most striking productions of colonial propaganda was the creation of '' Human Zoos '' from the beginning of the 19th century. The objective was to set up a spectacular device aimed at questioning the humanity of those who were exhibited, namely women, men, and children shown as '' savages '' at various events and in different configurations (fairs, gardens, theaters, zoos, etc.). At the end of the 19th century, these exhibitions and their coverage by the media had already imposed and anchored in minds the representations of the '' non-White '' populations as '' wild '' and '' primitive '', that it was necessary to '' civilize ''. Real mass shows, these human zoos played a major role in establishing the '' race '' as a model of understanding the world, engraving in the collective unconscious the idea that there would exist multiple '' Human Races '' that could be classified and hierarchized, with,

the direct colonization of the continent by Germany, Belgium, Spain, Italy, Portugal, the United Kingdom... This colonization will allow Europeans to plunder mineral, agricultural resources, as well as cultural objects and goods, etc.

The theories formulated by the colonisers will be widely disseminated among the Europeans present on the African continent, acting on behalf of their nations or in the context of missionary activities. For example, in 1903, in the German colony of Togo, the Prefect Apostolic of the Society of the Divine Word, Bishop Bücking, who had gone to visit associates arrested and imprisoned because of suspicions of intrigues against the circle commander of Atakpamé, was escorted by colored soldiers from the entrance of the city of Atakpamé to the prison. By filing his brief before the court of appeal in Douala, Father Franz Müller, a missionary of the same Congregation, expressed his displeasure at the fact that: '' Prefect Bücking was escorted three hours from Atakpamé by soldiers without Europeans ''. Moreover, describing the conditions of incarceration of Bishop Bücking's collaborators, he noted:

> It is a treatment devoid of any consideration and which causes much damage to the authori-

---

of course, the '' White Race '' in mind (A. M. Gossiaux, 2022, p. 32).

ty they so need. Their permanent surveillance by black soldiers, the inadequacy and inconvenience of the cells for the Europeans that they are, the use of dirty sheets and blankets with the exception of the Müller cell (cited by K. Adja, 2016, p. 9).

Franz Müller was shocked by the color of the skin of the people accompanying the Prefect and those responsible for monitoring European prisoners. For this German missionary, it represented a lack of respect and consideration for the White fathers. Is this not a confirmation of manifest anti-Black racism, even in ecclesiastical clothing? In 1884, when Togo had just been colonized by Germany, the Akposso, the Houdou, the Idaatcha, the Ifè, the Mahi, the Kabiyè, etc., constituted the socio-cultural groups present in Atakpamé. Research carried out by Togolese historians reveals that these peoples, established before the arrival of European colonizers, were able to develop remarkable political, economic, social, cultural and religious structures, without ever depending on any Western intervention (A. S. L. Adotévi, 1996; L. S. Adotévi, 1999; T. Assogba, 2006; A. Agossou, 2007; A. Dossou, 2007; K. Indre, 2007; N. Gayibor, 2011, p. 249-290; D. O. Olougbégnon, 2016; S. Kossou, 2017; T. K. A. Odah, 2021; D. J. Azonaha, 2024).

In a geographical environment where the Kingdom of Danxomè was a formidable enemy, the sociolinguistic communities of Atakpamé were able to contain an ambient insecurity by taking advantage of their natural resources, such as hills with caves to take shelter on one side, and by producing weapons (arrows, clubs, etc.) to resist the invader, thus demonstrating a spirit of solidarity and bravery. Consider that these human groups, and by extension all those who occupied Togo before colonization, were '' savages '' requiring a civilizational contribution from Europe, constitutes a mistaken vision of the history of these women and men who were able to maintain their existence with dignity and pride.

It is under the influence of the perceived superiority of Whites over Blacks that the White minority in South Africa will, during the first half of the 20th century, impose on the Black majority a policy of racial segregation referred to as apartheid. Established by the National Party in 1948, apartheid was in effect until 1991. According to Antoine Bouillon and Robert Archer (1981), this segregationist policy had considerable effects on sport in this country, insofar as the relationship between sport and Whites was a fundamental principle; sport being the privileged tool of Afrikaners to reaffirm their belonging to civilization, moreover Western.

In a desperate attempt to impose their cultural values, the Whites of South Africa have sought to erase from the minds of the Blacks their own past, which is rich in significant events and heroes. For example, Chaka Zulu is one of the figures that White colonization and apartheid have failed to remove from the collective memory of South Africa, and even Africa in general. In the extremely militarized society he managed to establish, he erected heroism as a fundamental value of Zulu ethics. A recognized hero enjoyed more political power than a prince of royal blood. This practice ensured equal opportunities for all those who came under its authority. Whoever joined his ranks to defend the interests of the Zulu People became Zulu himself, and many historical indications suggest that the majority of his generals and relatives were of foreign origin. The history of Chaka is intrinsically linked to the pre-colonial era, often reduced by colonial historians to a simple succession of insignificant exploits between opposing villages. Over time, the authentic image of Chaka has contradicted this prejudice: Chaka was truly a hero of an Africa that strove to transcend its clan and socio-cultural divisions just before the advent of colonial rule (K. I. Bosco, 1989, p. 46-47).

From the above, it is possible to assert that the prejudices of the Arab-Muslims and Europeans have allowed for the concocting of astounding theories, completely devoid of any reliable scientific basis, according to which the Black Man would be an entity without dignity, without history and without achievements, left adrift in a world that required a bit of civilization with regard to it. By deceiving themselves, the promoters of these dark reflections managed to persuade a large part of their compatriots. The repercussions were fatal and irrevocable: Slave Trades, colonization, segregation, forced labor, mandatory contributions to the two world wars, paternalistic relations between the West and the Black Continent[23], murders of political leaders unwilling to maintain the interests of the former Western colonial powers[24], among others, have constitut-

---

[23] For example, since the time of Charles de Gaulle, France has maintained very close relations with African political leaders and heads of state. At that time, there was a direct telephone line between the French president and some African heads of state. Moreover, Jacques Foccart had set up networks that managed appointments within the African political sphere, with the aim of safeguarding the sustainability of French influence (J. Ki-Zerbo, 2003, p. 50-51). Even more strikingly, Jean-Bedel Bokassa perceived himself more as the best ambassador of France in the Central African Republic than as the leader of a sovereign state. He did not hesitate to call Charles de Gaulle '' Papa '' - although the latter described him as a '' soudard '' - and then Valéry Giscard d'Estaing '' my dear relative '' or '' my cousin ''.

[24] For example, we can mention the tragic fate of Prime Minister Patrice Lumumba (1925-1961) of the Republic of the Congo (currently Democratic Republic of the Congo), whose assassination required the active intervention of Belgium, which consid-

ed the tragic menu of the history of African populations. At present, awake and aware, the Africans fully grasp all the deceptions orchestrated in their absence to strip them of their money and accuse them of sins for which they have never been guilty. Thanks to quality scientific research, Africans achieve one essential thing: they are not cursed! We are in no way cursed!

In the next chapter of this study, it is essential to highlight that Africa is identified, according to rigorous scientific research, as the cradle of all civilizations on our planet. This recognition is also reflected in the field of domestication of several plant species favorable to the survival and sustainability of Man, both on the African continent and beyond[25].

---

ered it an obstacle (D. Bacquelaine, F. Willems and M.-T Coenen, 2001).

[25] We are discussing agriculture, because without it, humans would not be properly fed and would risk an inevitable death. In a speech delivered on 6 September 1952, Adlaï Stevenson II (1900-1965), an American politician and member of the Democratic Party, declared : '' A man who is hungry is not a free man ''. Therefore, if human communities had been constantly starving, they would never have been able to establish organized sociopolitical entities. Without cooking, which represents a supreme art, and without food, Man simply would never have existed.

CHAPTER 2

Africa, between the emergence of the first *Homo sapiens* and the domestication of various plant species

In the second chapter of this study, It is demonstrated that the African continent, according to accessible and verifiable scientific data, is incontestably the original cradle of humanity, regardless of skin pigmentation. The occupation of African territories by *Homo sapiens* then leads to the domestication and spread of an incalculable number of plants essential for nutrition here and beyond.

2.1. Africa is the cradle of humanity!

For Joseph Ki-Zerbo (2003, p. 9), it is undeniable that the African continent is the cradle of humanity. On this subject, he claims that no one disputes him, even though many forget it: "I am sure that if Adam and Eve had appeared in Texas, we would hear about them every day on CNN", he says. Decades before this Burkinabè historian, to whom we paid a vibrant tribute during his centenary, through an international conference held in Cotonou on June 22 and 23, 2022[26], Théophile Obenga (1969), also known as Mwene Ndzale, strongly emphasized that paleoanthropological and archaeological discoveries have led researchers, mainly Western ones, to conclude that Africa is the first continent to have seen the emergence of Man[27].

For the Congolese historian and linguist, subsequently, groups of populations of African origin gradually occupied regions of the world outside the current Black Continent: Western Europe, for example, from the south of the Iberian Peninsula to Scotland, passing through the southeast of France. He emphasizes that it is recognized that the Mesolithic and Neolithic populations of Portugal (Tagus

---

[26] The Proceedings of the conference, published in 2023, are entitled *Ki-Zerbo. Hommage à l'occasion du centième anniversaire de l'historien.*

[27] For Mwene Ndzale Obenga (1969, p. 83) : '' It is quite difficult to accuse prehistorians, archaeologists, historians and intellectuals (...) (Arambourg, Dart and Leakey, Darwin and Weinert, Bosch-Gimpera, G. Hervé, R. Bailly, Giuffrida-Ruggeri and Peyrony, Breasted, Pericot Garcia, G. Childe and Mendes Correa, R. May and M. Saunier, Diodorus of Sicily and Strabo, etc.) to have been or to be individuals driven by an pride of race and people ''.

Valley) have characteristics specific to the Black Man. Obenga's claims are also supported by those of the mathematician and economist Yao Modzinou (2008, p. 17-18):

> The modern man called homo sapiens appeared in Africa and spread across the entire surface of the earth. Schematically, this swarm is generally presented on a map of the world with a legend about human migrations. As migrations, it would rather be, according to a large number of authors, small displacements within the frame-work of an economy of hunter-gatherers in which the scarcity of resources implies each time a change of place of life. Movements of this kind over a few hundred generations validly explain the occupation of the globe without necessarily being comparable to migrations in the sense we understand them today.

In his book *Petite histoire de l'Afrique. L'Afrique au sud du Sahara, de la préhistoire à nos jours*, the French historian Catherine Coquery-Vidrovitch (2016, p. 25-26) indicated that the ancestors of Man appeared on the Black Continent several million years ago. Since the early 1990s, the original home of humanity had been attributed to East Africa due to the discovery of the remains of a small woman named Dinknesh or Lucy and who would have lived some 3.5 million years ago. Dinknesh was discovered on 24 November 1972 at Hadar, on the banks of the

Awash River, in Ethiopia. However, this focus was questioned for two reasons: according to the first reason, it was established that Man does not come directly from Dinknesh which was only one of the many aborted branches of genetic mutations that gradually differentiated Man from the great apes. Dinknesh or Lucy, who could still climb trees, would be a kind of great-great-aunt Australopithecine left without descent.

As for the second reason, it was associated with the discovery of a fossilized skull called Toumaï (*Sahelanthropus tchadensis*) in the Djourah desert, in central Africa, Chad, in 2001. According to research based on biochronology, this vestige would have more than double the age of Dinknesh, that is to say 7 million years. Other studies even refer the fossil to 10 million years. The dating of 10 million years is not a simple coincidence, because it confers the title of the oldest ancestor of Man, in opposition to a fossil named Orrorin (*Orrorin tugenensis*), found in November 2000 in the hills of Tugen, in Kenya, in East Africa, which was dated at 6 million years.

Catherine Coquery-Vidrovitch (2016, p. 27) points out that in 2001 the trace of the world's first known cut stone tools was discovered in Tanzania, East Africa, going back 700,000 years before *Homo* appeared as a separate species. Moreover, the study conducted by the French researchers François Bon and

François-Xavier Fauvelle (2022, p. 17-19) indicates that in 1976, at the site of Laetoli in Tanzania, footprints alongside those of elephants, giraffes, and antelopes were found and dated to 3.66 million years ago. These footprints were left by several individuals of a bipedal primate species belonging to the genus Australopithecus. In 2009, in Kenya, similar footprints, dating back 1.52 million years, were discovered at Ileret, presenting a different foot morphology, thus revealing a locomotion similar to that of the Homo genera (*erectus*[28] or *ergaster*[29]).

In 2020, elephant footprints and human traces, probably those of *Homo sapiens* similar to current men and women, were found in the Nefad Desert in present-day Saudi Arabia, accompanied by footprints of elephants, wild dromedaries, and other herbivores. Dated between 121,000 and 112,000 years ago, these footprints constitute a clear manifestation of the dissemination of modern humans outside the African continent. In the 2010s, at Engare Sero, near Lake Natron in Tanzania, a group of several hundred footprints was unearthed, dated between 20,000 and 5,000 years before the Christian era. These traces materialize a path (the footprints, although following opposite directions, all share the

---

[28] A man standing, thus completely freeing his hands.

[29] A man of great stature, built for racing, which allows him to leave Africa.

same orientation). Some of them come from a group of 14 women all marching at an identical pace, accompanied by two men and a child. According to Bon and Fauvelle, these footprints testify to a predominantly female group engaged in the harvest of grasses, fruits, and tubers. They also have an undeniable importance: they emphasize that the key moments in the evolutionary history of humanity are now better preserved on the African continent than in other regions of the world. In other words, in the light of current knowledge, Africa remains unquestionably the original home of humanity[30]!

However, despite the scientific evidence set out above that Africa is the cradle of humanity, a tradition marked by racist prejudices has long propagated the idea that agriculture was only a relatively recent practice in sub-Saharan Africa. This perception, in addition to being accompanied by simplistic scenarios and a lack of understanding about the origin of many African cultivated species, has led to minimize, if not ignore, the essential role of the Black Continent in the development of agriculture on a global scale. In the second part of this chapter, we will briefly present this aspect while ensuring to question it, because solid research has shown that the Black Continent is indeed the cradle of a significant num-

---

[30] Read also Lilian Thuram (2014, p. 11-15).

ber of cultivated plants, which have spread to the rest of the world.

2.2. Africa, a cradle of plants cultivated both here and elsewhere

At the end of the 19th century, the French anthropologist Sigismond Zaborowski (1893, p. 529) declared, for example: "According to all the probabilities in sum, all of western, central and southern Africa was foreign to agriculture at the time of the discovery of America. And it was the relations established for the Slave Trade between it and the new continent that transformed it". The author also stated that: "If we removed from Black Africa what it was able to borrow from the civilizations of its Mediterranean coasts, more than 6000 years old, I do not know what would remain to it, nor even if something would remain to it. She probably never invented anything" (J.-M. Bergougniou, R. Clignet and P. David, 2001, p. 102). As a result, all or almost all cultural innovations were supposed to come from southwest Asia, first reaching the Nile valley and finally spreading to Africa (D. Clark, 1962, p. 211-228).

However, over time, research in archaeology, associated with paleobotany, will allow to nuance, then contradict these preconceived ideas inherited from colonialism: there is no ancient evidence of a systematic diffusion of cultural elements coming from the Near-Orient; on the contrary, numerous direct data (seeds, fossilized pollens, etc.) as well as complementary elements, such as agricultural and culinary tools, show that certain plants really have an African origin (P. J. Munson, 1976, p. 187-209).

Apart from the works by the Franco-Swiss botanist Alphonse Louis Pierre Pyrame de Candolle (1886, p. 11-12, 17), which were first published in 1883, it was only with the contributions of the Russian agronomist and geneticist Nikolaï Vavilov (quoted by D. A. Cissé, 1988, p. 169, 172 and 188) that, in the wake of the October 1917 Revolution, a global and synthetic approach to the development of natural environments and the management of their resources would emerge. By integrating systematic analyses of floristic and phytogeographical data with agro-botanical inventories and genetic studies, the researcher was able to definitively establish that Africa is one of the main prehistoric and historical agricultural cradles.

It is proposed that there are eight centres of origin for cultivated plants, three of which are considered secondary. Among these centres, only the Abyssinian is in Africa, while the Mediterranean centre also covers Europe, North Africa and Egypt, while showing '' cultigenic affinities '' with the Near East. From a theoretical point of view, the contribution of Nikolaï Vavilov on the identification of cultivated plants has proved extremely important. This first contributed to differentiate the concepts of foci or primary centers of variation, which are distinguished by a great diversity of plant forms, with a predominance of dominant characters. Then, this allowed to identify the areas of secondary variation, where there is an abundance of recessive characters that are masked in the focus of primovariation. Thus, the location and geographical distribution of these different foci have led to the identification of an agricultural cradle, while areas of secondary variation offer the possibility of identifying civilizations that have domesticated and transformed plants.

Regarding the center of botanical origin of a cultivated plant species, the French Roland Portères and Jacques Barrau (1980, p. 731) emphasized that: '' The area occupied by the possible wild relatives of a cultigene is often and clearly distinguished from that or those where, due to man, the appearance of plant cultigene occurred, resulting from domestication, selection, and its diversification ''. This research marked a significant advance compared to Candolle's work, which limited the origin of agriculture and domestic plants to three main foci: China, Southwest Asia with an extension towards Egypt, and America. As for the French agronomist Augustin Chevalier (1936, p. 27-45), he declares the existence of a nuclear agricultural zone in the inner loop of the Niger river.

In 1959, the American anthropologist George Peter Murdock (1959, p. 64-67) extensively examined the botanical factor in the history of Africa. He proposes the existence of an autonomous African center for domestication of plants: he refers to it as the '' Sudanese complex '' and places it in the region of Haut-Niger. According to him, this complex, whose origins date back to the period between 5,000 and 4,000 years before the Christian era, would have undergone no influence from any other center and would be at the origin of nearly twenty plants, among which we can mention fonio, African rice, sorgho, millet as well as various tubers.

According to some studies, this region was probably entirely covered by a vast forest at that time and did not present the environments known to accommodate seed crops, particularly cereals (R. Tourte, 2005, p. 27). It is therefore much further north that they will try to shed light on the emergence of graniculture, in the region of Dhar Tichitt, which was then considerably drier (but still wetter than at present). It was on the archaeological sites of this region that anthropologist Patrick J. Munson (1976, p. 189) carried out, between 1966 and 1968, a thorough analysis of possible stages in the domestication of plants and the formation of human communities (that it dates from approximately 2,000 to 400 years before the Christian era).

Its objective is to contradict the hypothesis of Murdock, who states that nearly 25 plants are domesticated in the upper valley of the Niger River, without external influence. Munson's research leads to the following conclusions:

- About 2,000 years before the Christian era, the region had rivers and freshwater lakes; annual rainfall was at least twice as high as today. The flora was still dominated by wild herbaceous species, which are linked to future African cultigens such as *Pennisetum*, *Digitaria*, *Sorghum* and *Echinochloa*;

- The oldest phase of the archaeological sequence examined (Akreijit: about 2,000 years before the Christian era) highlights stone tools and millstones, as well as ornamented pottery and rock art depicting wild animals. Hunting and fishing were predominant, and although seeds of wild grasses were used, it does not appear that domestication of the plants was clearly engaged. After a period of extreme drought between 2,000 and 1,500 years before the Christian era, the rains return, filling again lakes and rivers, and the populations will return.

It is from 1,500 years before the Christian era (phase Khimiya) that domesticated animals make their appearance, surrounded by a flora composed of *Pennisetum*, whether in the wild or already domesticated, *Cenchrus biflorus* and *Celtis integriflora*. Around 1,000 to 900 years before the Christian era (Chebka phase), the domesticated *Pennisetum* becomes predominant, while the *Cenchrus biflorus* decreases, but the *Brachiaria deflexa* (Guinea millet) continues to exist, as indicated by the traces left on the pottery and the percentages of seeds found during the excavations.

According to Patrick J. Munson (1976, p. 204), it is shown that seed crop agriculture in West Africa emerged in the Sahelo-Sudanese regions more than a millennium before the Christian era: the savannas are at the origin of most of the plants currently grown in forests. What should be remembered from this research, often contradictory, is that they undeniably validate the African origin of certain cultivated plants.

It is undeniable that the African continent has experienced unique agricultural advances, based on the domestication of its own plants, from which the rest of the world has benefited. Even if gathering and hunting have long been the basis of the subsistence economy in Africa, this cannot be considered as a sign of delay or "underdevelopment" premature, but rather as a consequence of an abundance and diversity of natural resources that grow naturally, without requiring considerable effort. This phenomenon of abundance and variety of food resources available has thus allowed African populations to live more serenely in their environments, without it being essential to transform these plants through domestication. The need to transform and domesticate resources will only arise in the economy with the decrease of natural resources, thus leading to the need to manage food heritage: domesticated plants will highlight the endogenous character of cultural civilizations in Black Africa (D. A. Cissé, 1988, p. 179-180).

Generally speaking, the studies conducted by Roland Portères and Jacques Barrau (1980, p. 730-733) will suggest the existence of four main foci of origin and diversification of cultivated plants in Africa:

The Central Mediterranean encompasses a set of cultivated plants typical of Mediterranean regions, including cereals such as wheat and barley, as well as edible legumes like *Cicer*, *Lens*, *Pisum*, *Vicia*... This highlights the close links between this centre and that of the Middle East. There are also Mediterranean cultigenes, including the olive tree (*Olea europea* L.) and the carob tree (*Ceratonia siliqua* L.). Some of these species are however endemic to Africa, such as the argan tree (*Argania sideroxylon* Roem.), a tree from Morocco that produces argan oil and gum. Egypt, with its obvious connections to the Middle East, has played a decisive role in the evolution of agriculture and livestock farming in northern Africa. It shares with the Syrian Near East the origin of an economically significant plant, the bersim or clover of Alexandria, *Trifolium alexandrinum* L. Although this African region in the central Mediterranean has not directly influenced the agricultural history of tropical Africa, it deeply marked the Sahara during the humid era, conducive to cultural and pastoral activities.

The Nilo-Abyssine focus includes the Nilotic and Abyssine sectors. It is the witness and relay of many influences from the Near East, tropical Asia and Black Africa. This focus is somewhat similar to the Near-Eastern center with cereals such as wheat, barley, and legumes like *Cicer*, *Lens*, *Pisum*, and *Vicia*; but it is particularly related to African centers with cultivated plants belonging to the genus Sorghum. It has also been shown that species from tropical Asia transited through this outbreak when they were introduced to Africa. However, this cluster has distinctive cultigens such as the Arabian coffee tree (*Coffea arabica* L.), the Abyssinian banana (*Musa ensete* I. F. Gmelin), the teff (*Eragrostis abyssinica* Schrad.) as well as the *Guizotia abyssinica* (L. f.) Cass.

The East African Centre is distinguished by the variety of differentiated sorghum derived from *Sorghum verticilliflorum* Stapf., as well as by penillary mils and millets, notably *Eleusine coracana* Gaertn, the sesames, etc. This outbreak should be considered as the extension of the Abyssal outbreak in the equatorial highlands.

The West African region is home to a variety of sorghum derived from Sorghum arundinaceum Stapf., as well as mils-penicillaires such as *Pennisetum pychnostachyum* Stapf. and Hubb., or the *P. Gambiense* Stapf. and Hubb. We also find finger mils with *iburu, Digitaria iburua* Stapf., and fonio *D. exilis* Stapf., as well as various types of rice. This region is divided into two main sectors: the tropical sector and the subequatorial sector. The tropical sector itself is divided into several subsectors: Senegambian, Interior Nigerian and Chadian-Nilotic. The Senegalese subsector is notable for its *sorghum* such as *Sorghum gambicum* Snowd and *S. cernuum* Host., as well as for its mils *Pennisetum psychnostachyum* Stapf, *P. nigritanum* Dur. and Sching., and *P. gambiense* S. and H. Also found are millets *Digitaria exilis* Stapf, *Brachiaria deflexa* C. E. Hubbard and oilseeds like

Polygala butyracea Heck. In the sub-sector of inland Niger, *Sorghum guineense* Stapf and *S. exsertum* Snowd, as well as mils *Pennisetum cinereum* S. and H. and geocarps *Kerstingiella geocarpa* Harms are widely represented. As for the Chadian-Nilotic sub-sector, it is distinguished by mils like *Pennisetum ancylochaete* S. H. and P. gibbosum S. and H., as well as oilseeds like *Ceratotheca sesamoides* Endl. and *Sesamum radiatum* Sch.

The subequatorial sector, on the other hand, is renowned for its production of cultivated yams, among which two species, *Dioscorea dumetorum* Pax and *D. cayenensis* Lamk., are particularly widespread, while sheltering a varietal group distinct from classical populations: *D. rotundata* Poir. In addition, this sector has contributed to the promotion of cultivars[31] such as *D. bulbifera* L., *D. macroura* Harms, seed-oil plants (*Elaeis guineensis* Jacq., *Telfairia occidentalis* Hook. f.) and plants with stimulant properties such as *Cola nitida* A. Chev.

The table below presents various domesticated species in Africa; it highlights the richness of the cultigens, their geographical distribution, their family affiliation, as well as data on their dating. Through this representation, one can grasp the importance of

---

[31] Cultivars : the term international is an abbreviation of '' cultivated variety '', that is to say a variety of plant.

the western part of the Black Continent in the transition from a predatory economy to a progressive production of resources. On a much smaller scale, notably in the '' Dahomey Gap '', the Beninese archaeologist Alexis Adandé (1993, p. 76) argues that:

> The domestication of plants, African species of yam probably from as early as -5000, in the forest-savannah contact area at the forest edge and, perhaps at the same time, that of the oil palm in the same ecological niche, were decisive factors in the emergence of agriculture in the '' Dahomey Gap ''. Some researchers even think that the Atakora Mountains may have been a '' secondary '' center for domestication of a variety of fonio (*Digitaria iburua*). Many other plants have been associated with these staple crops, pea bean (*Vigna unguiculata*), edible roots, Voandzou (*Voandzeia subterranea*).

The identification of domestication centers and cultivated varieties contributes today to a deeper, scientific, objective and enlightened understanding of the origins and itineraries of agricultural products grown on the African continent.

Table 1: *Some plants native to Africa.*

...tific Name	Common Name	Family	Place of Origin	Indic... sci...
Cereals				
...glaucum (L.) K. ...chum	Millet	Poaceae	Sahel, Darfour	Hogg... Dhar...
...corocana (L.)	Eleusinian	Poaceae	East Africa Ethiopia	Godel...
...ff (Zucc.) Trotter	Teff	Poaceae	East Africa Ethiopia	6th...
...lis stapf. Digitaria ...rua stapf	Fonio	Poaceae	Burkina Faso, Sierra Leone	Kam... n... Rim: 2...
Vegetables				
...culata (L.) Walp.	Cowpea	Fabaceae	Nigeria	
...jan (L.) Millsp.	Pigeon pea	Fabaceae	West Africa	

nnea (L.)	Bambara groundnut	Fabaceae	West Africa	
pa Harms	Geocarpa groundnut	Fabaceae	West Africa	
tus L.	Okra	Malvaceae	Tropical and Eastern Africa	
Stimulating plants				
a L.	Arabica coffee	Rubiaceae	Ethiopia	
a Pierre	Liberica Coffee	Rubiaceae	Ouganda and Congo	
a G. Don	Kola	Sterculiaceae	West Africa	
Fibers				
ceum L.	Cotton	Malvaceae	Tropical Africa	
L.) Gaertn.	Kapok	Malvaceae	West Africa	
Oilseeds				
cum L.	Sesame	Pedialicea	East Africa, Niger Valley	

yssinica (L.f) Cass.	Ramtil	Asteraceae	Ethiopia	
communis L.	Castor bean	Euphorbiaceae	East Africa	
uineensis Jacq.	Oil palm	Arecaceae	Equatorial and sub-Equatorial regions of West and Central Africa	
Roots				
cayenensis Lam. *rotundata* Poir	Yam	Dioscoreaceae	West Africa, Ethiopia	
esculentus N.E.Br	Kafir potato	Lamiaceae	West Africa, Ethiopia	
stenocarpa Harms	Bean	Fabaceae	West Africa	
Cucurbits				
iceraria (Molina) tandl.	Calabash, gourd or shady	Cucurbitaceae	Tropical Africa	
inatus (Thumb.) Mansf.	Watermelon	Cucurbitaceae	Tropical Africa	

	Melon	Cucurbitaceae	Tropical Africa	
ɔ L.	Melon	Cucurbitaceae	Tropical Africa	
ia L.	Cucumber from the Antilles	Cucurbitaceae	Tropical Africa	
Hook. f.	Oyster nut	Cucurbitaceae	East Africa	
Fruits				
licas L.	Tamarin	Fabaceae	East Africa	
ata L.	Baobab	Bombacaceae	Tropical Africa	
ca Del.	Desert date	Zygophyllaceae	Tropical Africa	

Sources: Judith Carney (2001, p. 379), J. W. Purseglove (1976, p. 302-305) and Souayibou Varissou (1992, p. 17-18).

It should also be noted that the currents of influence and diffusion related to plants have been mutually reciprocal between the African continent and other regions of the globe. These multiple influences have been integrated into the rich local heritage. Thus, due to human migrations, plants have continuously traveled from one continent to another. As a result, Africa has not only welcomed food and non-food plants from other continents, but also exported them. Let's take the example of Asia: Mesopotamia, Iran and India have received from the African continent the cultivation of sorghum. India, in particular, obtained cotton from Africa at a time when the latter was used as an oilseed rather than as a textile material. Many other varieties of African plants have been introduced into the New World.

These include bean (*Vigna unguiculata* L.), okra (*Hibiscus esculentus* L.), oil palm (*Elaeis guineensis* Jacq.), kola, sesame (*Sesamum indicum* L.), yam (*Discorea* spp.), watermelon (*Citrullus lanatus* T.) and earth pea (*Voandzeia subterranea* L.). The bean, referred to as Black-eyed peas or cowpeas by the Anglo-Saxons, was used by ships as food for slaves. This plant was introduced in Jamaica in 1674 and in the southern United States of America in 1738 (A. Adiko and A. Clérici, 1963, p. 24; D. A. Cissé, p. 178; R. Portères and J. Barrau, 1980, p. 741-742).

If there is an African plant that has become a true emblem in Louisiana and the southern United States of America, it is certainly the okra. Baudry des Lozières (1893, p. 308) expressed himself on this subject at the end of the 18th century in these terms:

> There are no softening substances used in chest ailments, which, in the colonies, are more numerous than those of the gum (...) All parts of the gum enter into stews of naturals from the colonies, and Europeans like the Creoles, find in the fruit of this small shrub, an excellent food.

The Anglo-Saxons call the okra plant, a term that would be of Ashanti origin. Ngombo is the name used by the Central African Bantu community to designate this plant. It was also introduced in Brazil before 1658, in Suriname before 1686, and in Barbados in 1750. Oil palm cultivation was documented in the 18th century in Jamaica and Martinique (J. Carney, 2001, p. 393).

According to Alfred Mondjannagni (1969, p. 115), the French naturalist Michel Adanson was the first to characterize in 1750 the oil palm and its main uses. However, as early as 1703, Jacquin, after observing this tree in the Antilles, attributed to it the name of *Elaeis guineensis* or Guinea olive, whereas the oil palm has its true origin in the Gulf of Guinea and that it was simply imported into the Antilles at the same time as the slaves during the Slave Trade. For many years after the abolition of the Slave Trade, a flourishing trade took place between Africa and Bahia, consisting of palm oil shipments. Large quantities of kola nuts were also trafficked regularly; they served as stimulants for enslaved and liberated Africans, who used to chew them all day. Moreover, certain varieties were essential for divination and to understand the will of the deities sought (P. Verger, 1969, p. 43).

It was in the 16th century that Portuguese explorers discovered sesame on the shores of Guinea to bring it to Brazil. Introduced to South Carolina in 1730, the seeds of this plant were used to produce oil. Used frequently as ration food, yam has been introduced to the West Indies, Brazil, South Carolina and Suriname (J. Carney, 2001, p. 394). During the transatlantic trade, the *Brooks*, a slave ship based in Liverpool during the 1780s, stood out for its well-known methods of placing slaves on board, and obtained on the coasts of West Africa supplies intended for the survival of the captives during the crossing. Among the crops supplied to Africans, there were generally about seven tons of yams and 20 tons of rice and dry beans (H. S. Klein and S. L. Engerman, 1976, p. 1220).

It should also be noted that a number of agricultural products have had an equally significant role in the foreign trade of the Kingdom of Danxomè, particularly in trade with European and American nations:

> The export items (of the said kingdom) are: cotton, almonds and palm oil, peanuts, sesame seeds, ivory, country fabrics, gourds, vegetable butter, kola nuts, yams, chili peppers and other spices. These products are mainly spilled in England, France, Germany and Brazil (Abbé P. Bouche, 1885, p. 199).

During the 16th century, the Kingdom of Alada established trade relations across the Atlantic with the Portuguese, whose ships carried food to feed slave cargoes sold at the Gold Coast, in Portugal, then, from 1540, in Brazil. On this subject, Garcia Mendes Castello Branco (1881, p. 27) indicates that in 1575, the Aïzo monarchy exported yams, palm oil, and other foodstuffs necessary for Slave Traders: '' Com o rei de Arda que está junto á Mina, que é nosso amigo, mandam lá resgatar escravos negros e marfim e panos d'algodão e azeite de palma e muitos legumes como inhame e ontros mantimentos. Sahem deste porto cada anno um e dois navios carregados disto arribo[32] ''.

---

[32] The translation in English reads : '' With our friend the King of Ardra, who is near Mina, we send to treat negro slaves, ivory, cotton loincloths, palm oil, and many vegetables like yam and other foods. Every year, there are two ships leaving this port in charge of what is indicated above '' (P. Verger, 1968b, p. 36).

In the 16th century, John L. Vogt (1973, p. 460) observes that the Portuguese transported from São Jorge da Mina, located on the Gold Coast, food such as rice, yams, bananas, and palm oil to feed slaves who were transferred to foreign territories: '' The normal fare for a slave in transit to Mina consisted of a daily ration of palm oil, yams, and occasionally a portion of rice and/or bananas ''. In 1744, the slave ship from Nantes, the *Reine de France*, carried 404 slaves from the coasts of West Africa to Santo Domingo. To ensure the smooth progress of the journey, he had to acquire 13,000 pounds of fresh produce, including rice, chickens and goats, at an estimated cost of 2,500 pounds in goods (H. S. Klein and S. L. Engerman, 1976, p. 1224).

The watermelon was introduced to Florida in 1576 and to Brazil in 1648. As for the cultivation of earth pea, its appearance was noted in Suriname in 1770, and it persisted until the 1970s (J. Carney, 2001, p. 393-394). In the 18th century, particularly in 1795, Captain Eyriès (cited by S. Berbain, 1942, p. 95) reported that a large number of foods were produced and consumed on the islands of São Tomé and Príncipe. However, part of this production was intended to supply the slave ships calling in this area. On this subject, the French captain observes that the foodstuffs necessary for the supply of the vessels included: '' Coco, magat, bananas, corn, weight (peas), ris (rice), potatoes, yams, fruits and quantity of vegetables of all species ''.

Specifically, it is relevant to note that the African species of rice, *Oryza glaberrima* Steudel[33], which was at the center of our research for the Master's degree (2007), the DEA[34] (2009) and the Doctorate (2013), has been identified in Europe, more precisely on the Iberian Peninsula. This plant, recognizable mainly by the reddish hue of its caryopsis, was mentioned in Al-Andalous (Andalusia) by Andalusian agronomists and nutritionists from the 11th and 12th centuries (V. Lagardère, 1996, p. 76; A. A. Vido, 2015, p. 291-292). At a time when transatlantic trade was not yet established, the presence of this African plant species in Spain could be explained by the influence of the Arabs who exercised their domination in the region between the 8th and 15th centuries CE. Already present in sub-Saharan Africa due to the Muslim Slave Trade, they would probably have played an important role in the introduction of African rice grown in Spain by transiting through North Africa.

The species *Oryza glaberrima* was also spotted in Portugal during the 15th century. During this peri-

---

[33] On the origins of the plant, read Arthur Vido (2021a, p. 111-118).

[34] Diploma of Advanced Studies.

od, and even well before it, the country had to face various challenges, such as declining agricultural incomes and epidemics (in 1348, 1356, 1384, 1415, 1423, 1432, 1435, 1437-1438, 1458, etc.), which had demographic, economic, social, monetary and political. To counteract the decline in cereal production and, in particular, to ensure that towns are supplied with bread, a regular import policy has been introduced, with gradual intensification. As a result, Portugal has established direct commercial relations oriented towards the supply of cereals with Africa, England, Spain, France, Italy and the Germanic world. Due to food shortages, Lisbon imported rice varieties of the glaberrima species from the West African coast during the years 1498, 1506, 1510 and 1514 (A. H. de Oliveira Marques, 1998, p. 81-84; J. Carney, 2005, p. 336).

Africa has offered the Asian continent cultivated African rice. The Arabs, returning from the eastern coasts of Africa and native to Mecca, Yemen, and the Persian Gulf, are said to have carried with them the species *Oryza glaberrima*, which they then introduced into Asia. Historical evidence suggests that Africans also played a role in the spread of this cereal across North Africa to Asia. A notable event in the history of the Mali Empire could support this hypothesis: the pilgrimage to Mecca by Mansa Kankou Moussa in 1324. Enthroned, the manding king made this journey to the religious capital of Islam with 60,000 porters, 10,000 subjects, and 500 servants. The emperor carried on about forty mules more than two tons of gold in the form of canes or powder, which he distributed to the officers, officials and nobles of the court of the sultan of Egypt (T. N'Diaye, 2008, p. 60). His procession undoubtedly needed provisions to undertake this historic journey, famous for the unprecedented luxury displayed by the sovereign. It is conceivable that African rice, well known to the populations of the time, constituted one of the essential food elements to support the imperial delegation until its arrival. One can also mention the Askia Muhammad Touré, who, to make his pilgrimage to Mecca in 1496 and visit Egypt, had to travel with a strong representation and supplies (O. Kane, 2003, p. 12; A. Vido, 2014, p. 81-84).

As a result, like other continents, Africa has not been excluded from international trade. On the contrary, it presents itself as a set of authentic cultural cradles and as a world center of diffusion for certain species of cultivated plants, which ensure the survival and sustainability of humanity.

In the third and final chapter of this study, it is crucial to inform the reader about the implementation of various elements specific to Africa, without external influences, notably those of European and Arab-

Muslim origin. The practices addressed in this section mainly focus on medicine, democracy, as well as hygiene (oral, physical and environmental), which have generated in the Black Man a total and intrinsic absence of inferiority complex regardingwith regard to the White Man or the half-caste.

CHAPTER 3

The analysis of some elements particular to the African continent or the absence of a feeling of inferiority towards the White Man

This chapter highlights the fact that medicine, mathematics, and computer science have constituted recognized scientific fields widely practiced by Dark-Skinned individuals. This knowledge has offered them the possibility of building societies free from any inferiority complex towards people of other skin tones.

3.1. Medicine, mathematics and computer science: African scientific practices

In the article entitled *Médecine, pharmacopées traditionnelles et développement en Afrique*, E. Elom-Ntouzo'o (1978, p. 38-39) demonstrates that for the

African, since immemorial times, medicine results from a permanent reflection and questioning on the enigma that life and death raise, accompanied by its ardent desire to extend as much as possible life, this most precious good. This indicates that medicine and pharmacopeia are undoubtedly contemporary with the appearance of Man on earth, in response to numerous hostile forces whose sole purpose was to destroy him and who forced him, by force of circumstances, to seek means of protection and defense such as shelters and various weapons to deter, respond to aggression, and attack. In his analysis, the author, who is also an expert at the World Health Organization (WHO), states that Africa is one of the oldest lands of medical remedies and practices, if not the oldest. The valley of the Nile, where the priests of Memphis and Thebes practiced, saw the passage of a large number of Greek scholars who came to learn the secrets of the art of healing from the Africans. Moreover, the oldest Egyptian papyrus, dating from 1,500 to 2,000 Before the Common Era (BCE), bear witness to this.

It is widely acknowledged that in Africa, an authentic and scientific medicine has always coexisted, both in its conception and in its methods and techniques. Indeed, in his doctoral thesis in medicine, Pascal Hennequin (2001) shows that in Egypt, during the Pharaonic era, doctors played a crucial role in child health and hygiene. By relying on sources such as medical, literary or administrative papyrus as well as objects or bas-reliefs from monuments, the author managed to divide childhood into two distinct phases. The first is dedicated to neonatal and infant care, where breastfeeding constitutes a fundamental element. Doctors tried to prioritize this practice by means of medico-religious rites and remedies recorded in medical papyrus. Other treatments were also used for diseases whose causes remained obscure, such as those related to the *bââ* substance or to the *temyt* disease. Certain conditions affecting young children were already well identified, such as coughing, urinary retention, coryza or otitis.

Subsequently, a second phase extended from withdrawal to adolescence. The young Egyptian then benefited from an education aimed at instilling the moral values necessary to become a good Egyptian citizen. In addition to writing and reading, he acquired mastery of various sciences. Moreover, daily life was characterized by physical activities and games. At this stage, physicians applied their expertise to treat conditions such as diarrhoea, parasitic infections, ophthalmic diseases, as well as bites and trauma.

Regarding the introduction to medical sciences in Pharaonic Egypt, Diodorus of Sicily (cited by P. Hennequin, 2001, p. 60-61), a Greek historian from the 1st century before the Christian era, states: '' They are the only people who forbid people to practice a profession different from the one handed down to them by their parents ''. Medical education was therefore devolved to families or elders. Aspiring doctors used to go to houses of life associated with temples, which did not really resemble schools, but rather *scriptorium*. These places gathered together priests, doctors and scholars who came to study and copy the writings preserved in these institutions.

In reality, the transmission of medical knowledge from father to son was not exclusive to the ancient Egyptians. For example, in the Kingdom of Sahé founded by the Hueda, located in present-day Benin, knowledge and skills in medicine were also transmitted. According to the observations of the French traveler, the Chevalier des Marchais (quoted by J.-B. Labat, vol. 2, 1730, p. 165): '' Fathers leave their knowledge to the eldest of their children, after having demanded a solemn oath about what they hold most sacred, that they will never declare it ''. Well before the capture of the capital of this political entity by the Danxomè army, under the reign of *Dada* Agaja (1711-1740), which occurred in March 1727, the Chevalier des Marchais had declared that:

> We must not forget that there are Negro doctors and surgeons who, without having had their courses nor donned the robe of Rabelais, do not

> allow themselves to make cures of which our esculapes of Europe would be infinitely honored. They know simple admirables, whose juices, leaves, or barks are incredible cures (cited by J.-B. Labat, vol. 2, 1730, p. 164-165).

In his travelogue, the Chevalier des Marchais informs us that it was particularly difficult for a foreigner, and especially a European, to access any information concerning plants and other products used in the treatment of diseases:

> They make it a mystery that nothing in the world is able to penetrate. They are not asked to use them for the Whites, but they take extreme care to disfigure them in such a way that it is impossible to recognize them. The Knight of the M. had formed a close friendship with one of these doctors, in the thought of discovering someone of his secrets; he gave him gifts, he made him drink, he made him several times very advantageous offers, without having ever been able to get anything out of them; they would rather let themselves be killed than to discover nothing (cited by J.-B. Labat, vol. 2, 1730, p. 165).

In the periodical *L'Almanach noir*, for the months of April, May and June 1938, it is reported that a French Catholic father, having resided for a long period in Black Africa, expressed his displeasure at not having acquired any knowledge about medicine in this region of the world:

For the good reason that indigenous medical science remains secret among Black fetishers and doctors; they themselves acquired it during a long and painful learning. Their parents were careful to send them, very young, to some indigenous community deep in the bush where, over several years and a large number of initiations, these candidate-healers learned with songs and ceremonies, the useful use of certain leaves, of certain roots, of certain barks. They alone know in which determined cases it is necessary to use them either for decoctions or for poultices and since, once returned to public life, this knowledge constitutes their livelihood, they carefully refrain from communicating it to non-initiates: moreover they are bound by oath to keep these secrets and the slightest indiscretion would expose them to death (*L'Almanach noir*, 1938, p. 61).

Before the foundation of Danxomè by the *Agasuvi*, medicine was already booming on what is today known as the plateau of Abomey. Health practitioners, whether Yoruba, Aja, Hueda or Wéménu, intermittently occupied this geographical space between the 9th and early 17th centuries, attracted by its advantageous characteristics. Indeed, this geomorphological unit was protected by natural boundaries which, like true ramparts, made access difficult and made it a place of refuge. In addition to this natural asset contributing to the safety of the Abomey plateau, the biogeographical conditions gave it a notable healthiness and agreeableness. Famous practitioners of medicinal sciences, in search of freedom, were attracted to this place, which represented a pole of knowledge.

The health professionals maintained close ties with the members of pre-*Aladaxonu* society, knowing each one deeply and holding in their hands the most delicate threads of their existence. They followed the individuals from the uterine phase until the last minute of their terrestrial life. During the conception period, they ensured the protection of mothers and children by informing pregnant women of the risks associated with their condition and the preventive measures to adopt in order to promote a childbirth without great difficulties. They sometimes intervened when complications occurred during birth. After deliverance, it was the health professional who determined the spiritual personality of the individual through the elaboration of his hierogram of the *Fa*, and traced to him the orthonormal space in which he had to evolve to lead a pleasant earthly existence. Later on, when adolescence came, the doctor prescribed remedies to ensure reproduction and that the offspring were physically healthy (A. Dègbèlo, vol. 1, 1993, p. 40-41, 47).

Following the progressive domination of the Abomey plateau by the *Agasuvi* and the foundation of Danxomè, the practice of medicine has never ceased to be ensured by specialists renowned for their competence in this field. For example, childbirth, which was previously the prerogative of menopausal women, had begun to include multiparous women, known for their bravery: women who had had three to four children were trained in this practice. In general, four midwives assisted the roture women during labor. With regard to queens in labor, from the reign of Kpengla (1774-1789), the number of their attendants during childbirth was stipulated and reduced to two. A private house was also built for this purpose, in the palace, within the queens' district. The woman of the roture delivered at her home. While one of the young assistants massaged her kidneys with a large band, cut from *Botoyi*[35], and the second provided her with air, a menopausal woman, known for her ability to tell funny stories, entertained her, while another, very austere, observed the progress of work. It was the latter who attended the birth of the child (A. Dègbèlo, vol. 2, 1993, p. 485-486).

In the Kingdom of Danxomè, it is important to note that the King counted among his servants health

---

[35] *Botoyi* is a coarse, robust fabric made from warp cotton yarns combined with weft raffia yarn. This material was intended for the disadvantaged classes. The term '' Bo '' means '' in the meantime '', while '' to yi '' translates as '' take ! ''. The elites of society, for their part, preferred imported canvases.

agents designated under the term *Kpamègan* in *fongbé*. General practitioner, the *Kpamègan* was never specialized in a specific area of disease treatment. Therefore, his versatility allowed the sovereign not to surround himself with a large number of therapists whose reliability would be difficult to establish. The main selection criterion for the *Kpamègan* was above all related to his skills in occult sciences, as well as his ability to predict and treat diseases. These skills were understood and recognized by all. An expert in the field of occultism and healing could become or become *Kpamègan* in three ways: either he had already been in the service of a King and thus found himself under the authority of his successor if the latter decided so, after evaluating the effectiveness and loyalty of his services with his predecessor. He could also volunteer for the new King, who could eventually choose him from many candidates. Finally, this King could deliberately choose his *Kpamègan* apart from the volunteers, being of course fully aware of this.

The status of *Kpamègan* was not hereditary. In principle, a person was *Kpamègan* for life. However, there could be a cessation of this status if the new King chose not to renew the old *Kpamègan*. It was then that he selected his own doctor. Nevertheless, the previously serving *Kpamègan* could operate in the shadows and support the King's new choice. In reality, each *Kpamègan* was assisted by collaborators he knew and had chosen to help him in various responsibilities. These teammates were referred to as *Kpamèvi.*

The first daily duty of the *Kpamègan* was to go to the palace in the morning, where he was invariably welcomed with kindness. He was housed in a separate cell from the King's bedroom. He stayed there until the latter woke up and came to join him. He then took care to inquire about the King's state of health as well as any other health concerns that he considered necessary to bring to his attention. They exchanged words as long as the King desired. At the end of their conversation, a cannon shot signaled to the people the good awakening of the King.

The *Kpamègan* even accompanied the Monarch on military campaigns. It should be noted that during these campaigns, the *Kpamègan* was always received by the Sovereign from dawn for the reasons previously mentioned. Moreover, the King could call his personal physician at any time of the day; reciprocally, he was free to go to the King whenever he wished, for he was a trusted man to whom the King confided without hesitation. He also took care of the King's family. The latter provided him with resources and all that was necessary for him to carry out his mission (A. F. Iroko, A. Vido and C. Atchamou, 2019, p. 94-97).

Healthy soldiers received appropriate care during the military campaigns of Danxomè, while the war wounded were not neglected. According to the Beninese historian Abiola Félix Iroko (2025, p. 105-110), they benefited from meticulous care from the royal authority, which had set up an efficient system of care, administered by doctors specialized in this care. On the battlefield and up to Agbomè (often awkwardly called Abomey), the wounded were regularly followed intensively until their total recovery, for those who had survived.

In Danxomè, the Kings implemented a sanitary policy in favor of their subjects. This multifaceted approach encompassed both secular and religious elements. For the Sovereigns, this policy represented a major challenge, to the point that they gave it particularly marked attention. Indeed, the way in which their contemporaries and posterity evaluated their reign largely depended on the degree of happiness or unhappiness encountered by the subjects during their governance; health, an essential component of well-to be, could be compromised by natural factors beyond the King's control or decisions. However, since subjects judged the reign in terms of prosperity or calamity, depending on a positive or negative health balance, it also became a significant concern for the King (A. F. Iroko, 2002, p. 4).

In the Gulf of Benin, located in West Africa, circumcision, perceived as a minor surgical operation, had been carried out since time immemorial. In evoking the application of this intervention in the Kingdom of Sahé, the Chevalier des Marchais (quoted by J.-B. Labat, vol. 2, 1730, p. 159), a traveling writer of the first half of the eighteenth century, stated the following: '' The most skillful and the most spiritual do not know who has established its use among them, let alone the time and reasons for this establishment. When pressed on this article, they reply that their fathers and grandfathers saw it practiced for their ancestors, and since they practiced it, they must also practice it, and instruct their children ''.

As regards the anteriority of the operation, Cheick Anta Diop (1980, p. 64) points out: "Among the countless identical cultural facts in Egypt and in today's Black African world, we will only retain circumcision and totemism". We corroborated the claims of the Senegalese scholar in a recently published article, in which we clearly showed that circumcision in the sub-Saharan region has not been influenced by any Judeo-Christian or Muslim currents (A. A. Vido and K. R. Kouassi, 2025, p. 165-166).

Our research on circumcision also revealed that during the period between the 16th and 19th centuries, surgical intervention was carried out no earlier than eight days after the birth of the boy. This age presents ideal conditions for surgery, as studies have shown that one of the essential elements for clotting, vitamin K, reaches its normal level in the blood only between the fifth and seventh days after birth. On the third day, prothrombin exists only at about 30% of normal, whereas from the eighth day onwards it is higher than at any other time in a child's life: up to 110% of normal (Watch Tower Bible and Tract Society, vol. 1, 1997, p. 482). Therefore, strict compliance with the recommendations transmitted by the ancestors significantly reduced the risk of bleeding during surgery.

To conclude this section, it should be recalled that previous research has shown that circumcision is a proactive method of protection against sexually transmitted infections (Dr. Claparède, 1861, p. 15, 17 and 18); which suggests that the population of the Gulf of Benin probably resorted to this practice as an adjunct to the prevention of these infections.

On the African Continent, mathematics constituted a discipline largely integrated into the daily life of the populations, notably through calculation games, such as the *Awalé* or the *Aji* in *fongbé*. Well before the colonial period, the *Aji* is played with an apron, marbles, and pieces of bone. The apron is usually made of earth, although it can also be found in soft stone or metal, but most often a wooden tray with a rectangular shape is used, carefully designed. It can also take the form of a trough, a boat or an arch, supported or not by sculptures representing human bodies or animals. This apron consists of 12 cells organized in two parallel rows, sometimes with two additional cells (not used during the part) located at the ends, reserved for the grains, all having an ellipsoidal or rectangular shape. It is in the first 12 cavities that the seeds are placed in groups of four, at the beginning of the game.

The marbles, still 48 in number, can be made of seeds, stones, shells, etc. In general, those that are most often used come from the fruits of *Caesalpinia crista* or its variant *Caesalpinia bonducella*, named *Ajikwin* in *fongbé*. Regarding the pieces of wood, there are two that are used for counting. Note that the game is elimination with 3 goals (3-0, 3-1, 3-2) and that the arrangement of the pieces allows reading the score:

1-0: the late player places one of the pieces in front of him;

1-1: each player places one of the pieces in front of them, but the heads oriented in opposite directions;

2-0: the two pieces are arranged in front of the late player, the heads in the same direction;

2-1: the two pieces are positioned in front of the late player, the heads opposite;

> 2-2: the two pieces are removed, as if one were at 0-0, which is called *Ajibègo* (the game, *Aji*, has seized the knot, meaning that: the game is demanding) and the suspense settles.

Aji is a single-cycle game where sowing occurs in the trigonometric direction. The game can include several rounds. After a uniform distribution of pawns in the cavities, a draw is carried out, and the two players take turns. For each move containing a single seed, the player retrieves the content of the finish box if it contains one or two seeds. The same applies to the previous boxes, provided they continuously have one of the contents mentioned. However, it is a minor game; the real challenge is to calculate and accumulate, in a personal pot, a sufficient number of pawns to capture a significant part of them in the opposing tiles by completing several turns on the board. With this in mind, the player must force his opponent to empty his hand so that no more than one pawn remains in the targeted pots.

This move is often decisive for the outcome of the game. Nevertheless, when two experts confront each other, the opponent's intentions are quickly perceived and a counter-strategy is implemented. This preparation is thought out well in advance; to succeed, it is imperative to recognize the opponent's intentions and play accordingly. Counter-strategy can be offensive or defensive. In the first case, we increase the contents of the opponent's accumulation pot until it becomes unusable. Defensive counterstrategy consists of maintaining stop pots or knots (*ebla go* in *fongbé*) containing at least two pieces (in order to counter accumulations), which makes the grain null or poor.

The order established in the game stems from certain rules that govern it. In addition to some rules already mentioned (such as the direction of the game), any player capable of completing a full turn on the board must skip the starting locker: it is said that he has created a house. Subsequently, as long as possible, the player must provide pawns to his opponent: in other words, give him something to eat. Any player who violates this requirement, monopolizing all the pawns on their side and preventing the other from playing, is punished: their opponent collects for their benefit all the pawns present on the board. Moreover, a player cannot afford to capture all the pawns of the other side. Among the last two rules, the first imposes solidarity, and the second fight against selfishness; this is particularly evident in social interactions. The *Aji* game ends when there is no more combination possibilities, due to the insufficient number of pawns. Consequently, each player adds his catches to what remains in his camp by filling each locker with four marbles; the gain is determined by the number of pawns remaining when there are no pots left to fill (Ch. Béart, 1955, p. 475-516).

According to the Beninese anthropologist Félix F. Hodonou (1989, p. 95-106), a detailed analysis of the *Aji* game reveals the use of mathematical concepts such as combinatorial analysis and its various permutations, probabilities, and so on. For his part, Marc Chemillier (2008, p. 6, 8) points out that this strategic game is a subject conducive to the examination of reasoning mechanisms, insofar as it evolves in an abstract framework made of boxes and pawns, distinct from the real world, with clearly defined rules. It incorporates into its fundamental structure the notion of sequentiality (regular alternation of moves) which creates a link with the linear scheme of deductive reasoning ('' if I play this, then it happens"). Based on research conducted by ethnomathematicians, the French anthropologist demonstrated that certain series of blows generated stable configurations (which repeated indefinitely), while others followed each other periodically. This suggests that experienced African players were aware of these characteristics and integrated them into their strategies.

It is well established that the Great Wall constituted a set of military fortifications in China, built, destroyed and rebuilt several times and in various places between the third century BC and the seventeenth century after the Christian era, with the aim of symbolizing and protecting China's northern border. According to the writings dealing with this theme, it is considered as the most significant architectural structure ever created by humanity, both in length, area and volume[36]. However, a less well-known fact, which should be brought to the attention of Africans, is that there once existed in present-day Nigeria a kingdom called Benin, founded in the 11th century CE. The capital of this political entity was Benin City.

In 2016, an article in the *Guardian* highlighted the magnificence of the capital. The British newspaper reported that the 1974 Guinness Book of Records described the walls of Benin City as the world's largest earthworks before the advent of the mechanical era. According to estimates by the British journalist and author Fred Pearce of the New Scientist, at one point the walls were '' four times longer than the Great Wall of China and used a hundred times more materials than the Great Pyramid of Khufu ''. Pearce indicates that these walls:

> extended over some 16,000 km in total, in a mosaic of more than 500 interconnected colony boundaries. They covered 6500 km² and were

---

[36] Cf. https://www.beauxarts.com/grand-format/la-grande-muraille-de-chine-dragon-de-pierre-aux-mille-et-une-vies/. Visited on February 15, 2026 at 1 : 40 PM.

all dug by the Edo people... It is estimated that they took 150 million hours to build and that they constitute perhaps the largest archaeological phenomenon on the planet[37].

Given that architecture is in fact a direct application of geometry, algebra and trigonometry in design and structuring, it is clear that the founding people of the Kingdom of Benin had extensive mathematical knowledge. The fields of mathematics mentioned above allowed them to calculate loads, model shapes, optimize materials, ensure stability, and incorporate aesthetic principles.

It is recognized that computer science represents not only a science, but also an art and technique of systematic and logical processing of information. According to the French Academy (April 1966), it is defined as '' the science of rational processing, notably by automatic machine, of information considered as support for human knowledge and communications in technical, economic and social fields '' (quoted by J. Nlandu Ngunda, 2024, p. 2). In this scientific discipline, the act of writing instructions for a computer is referred to as coding or programming.

---

[37] Cf. https://artkarel.com/tag/anatomie/. Visited on February 15, 2026 at 7 : 43 PM.

Technically, coding corresponds to an operation that establishes a correspondence between information and a sequence of " 0 " and "1 " representable by machines. Among the most well-known and widely used coding systems, ASCII (American Standard Code for Information Interchange) stands out as being the most widespread. This code works on 8 bits, thus allowing to define $2^8 = 256$ distinct binary combinations, which allows the encoding of 256 characters (26 lowercase letters, 26 uppercase letters, 10 digits, 10 syntactic symbols, as well as accented characters such as ù, à, è, é, â... and semigraphic characters) (J. Nlandu Ngunda, 2024, p. 10).

It is essential to note that this coding has been present in Africa since very ancient times and manifests itself through divination known as *Ifa* in *yoruba* and *Fa* in *fongbé*. *Fa* is one of the divination systems used in West Africa, particularly in Nigeria, Benin and Togo. This system is based on a set of signs called *Du*, which are presented graphically by two groups of parallel and vertical lines, transcribed and readable from right to left on four columns. The *Bokonon* in *fongbé*, also called *Babalawo* in *yoruba*, is the priest of *Ifa* or *Fa*, and he interprets the *Fa Du* (the divisions of *Fa*) through the divinatory chain, which can be performed with rope or metal. In total, there are 16 *Fa Du* cardinals, which give birth to 240 others, bringing the total to 256. These Cardinals' *Fa* are referred to as *Méji*, meaning '' two '' in *yoruba*, and are formed by a repetition of the same sign (M. Kakpo, 2021, p. 165-175; A. M. Akodigna and A. A. Vido, 2017, p. 55).

According to Stefania Capone (2018, p. 173), the *Fa* relies on a binary logic for its divination system. This has led some Nigerian authors to regard it as a language largely preceding ASCII, which was adopted as the computer standard in the 1960s and allows 8-bit character encoding, thus producing 256 possible characters. As with the *Du* in *Fa* divination, each character is associated with an eight-digit combination, by virtue of binary logic.

From what has been mentioned, it is possible to observe that human societies, which European intellectuals have designated as '' primitive '', have given rise to divinatory techniques that have been developed with a thorough mastery of their environment, while adopting a truly scientific approach (M. Chemillier, 2008, p. 31-32).

The scientific knowledge held by people with Black Skin proves that they have been endowed with remarkable skills capable of building societies that are both sustainable and free from any inferiority complex. These women and men will show behaviors characteristic of individuals with exceptional civilizational values, deserving of a thorough analysis.

3.2. The feeling of inferiority towards the White Man or the half-breed, an element absent from African psychology of the pre-colonial period

For a long time, Dark-Skinned people have worked to build societies in sometimes hostile contexts. To preserve their achievements and ensure a lasting legacy, it was essential for them to control their interests at the political, economic, socio-cultural, religious and other levels. To achieve this goal, they were willing to resort to all possible strategies, including alliances, trickery, and even murder, among others. This approach was carried out without ever letting oneself be overwhelmed by a feeling of inferiority in the face of a community or the color of their skin. The absence of any manifestation of the inferiority complex towards the Whites is amply documented and experienced in the history of the Kingdom of Danxomè, for example.

In 1727, when King Agaja managed to seize the capital of the Kingdom of Sahé, his immediate goal was to control the city of Gléhué, which is awkwardly referred to as Ouidah. His soldiers launched an attack on the maritime province, capturing many prisoners, including several Europeans present on the coast at that time. According to the testimony of the Englishman Guillaume Snelgrave (1735, p. 18-21), who arrived at Gléhué a few days after Sahé was taken by Agaja, it is noted that: "The soldiers of Dahomè (...) made (prisoners) forty other Whites, both English, French, Dutch and Portuguese (...) The day after the capture of the city of Sabée, the Whites made prisoners were sent to the countryside, to the king of Dahomè (...) A few days later, they were handed over in freedom, and they were sent to the Fort of the English and the French".

It is important to note that for *Dada* Agaja, the capture of Whites as prisoners does not date back to the military campaign against the Hueda, but rather to that against the Aïzo of the Kingdom of Alada. When the monarch's forces penetrated the capital of Alada on 30 March 1724, their objective was to conquer it. This situation led to the destruction of Togudo, as reported by Bulfinch Lamb, an English employee of the *Royal African Company*, who was captured in the city during the fighting and then sent to Agbomè where he stayed for some time (G. Smith, 1, 1751, p. 116-123).

In his manifest intention to appropriate Gléhué, in March 1727, Agaja clashed with Oyo, who was visibly displeased to see the Fon King occupying part of the coast without his consent. The King of Oyo ordered a punitive operation against the Fon country in order to force it to submit. Furthermore, Oyo strongly encouraged the Hueda to fight to take back their territory from Agaja. It is in this context that Testefole, then at the head of the British Fort of Gléhué, also chooses to support the Hueda. Deeply committed to their uprising, he repeatedly threatened King Agaja, whom he held responsible for the insolent behavior of his representatives in Gléhué. He would not have hesitated to suffer the consequences of his reckless words. In August 1729, Agaja attacked Gléhué, cruelly repressed the Hueda and had Testefole captured. The Englishman was sent to Agbomè, where he was subjected to atrocious tortures before being decapitated (C. Savary, 1976, p. 26; A. Zohou, 2021, p. 46).

In 1730, a treaty was concluded between Danxomè and the supreme authority of Oyo. The Yoruba incursions against Danxomè were interrupted[38]. The Fon King then set about protecting his new hueda possessions (A. Vido, 2021b, p. 496-498). In 1731, the King of the Hueda, Houffon, wanted to start negotiations with Agaja to reoccupy his territory, but he changed his mind after receiving advice from Mynheer Hendrick Hertog, who was then an agent of the Dutch West India Company and who offered him his support. Other attempts to restore the Kingdom were

---

[38] At that time, Danxomè, in order to ensure peace, was forced to pay annual tributes to Oyo.

launched, but they all failed. These struggles of resistance, however, had the effect of slowing down commercial activities in Gléhué due to the instability that prevailed there. The European slave ships had to face the consequences of this resistance. Indeed, according to Joâo Basilio (quoted by P. Verger, 1965, p. 41), who was director of the Portuguese Fort of Gléhué from 1728 to 1743, the Hueda troops, supported by Hertog, carried out looting and killed two Portuguese slain. Another slave ship that tried to enter the harbor of Gléhué was also massacred.

This situation led Agaja to consider with great seriousness Hertog's opposition towards him, turning it into a personal matter. He launched an offensive against Jakin, where the Dutchman had taken refuge in April 1732, but the latter managed to escape and hid at Ekpè. Agaja then forbids any form of communication with this locality, in particular with Hertog, on pain of death. All the Dutch became targets of his resentment towards Hertog. To escape the numerous attacks orchestrated by Agaja against him, Hertog was forced to leave Ekpè to take refuge further east, in Gbadagri (now Nigeria), in 1736, from where he continued to incite unrest against the interests of Danxomè. He will finally be caught unprepared and executed by henchmen of Agaja in this same city during a raid on April 29, 1738 at 7: 30 PM (N. L. Gayibor, 1990, p. 100-101).

During the reign of Kpengla (1774-1789), one of the sons of *Dada* Agaja, Danxomè, for mainly economic reasons, proceeded to arrest some European merchants who were then incarcerated in the prisons of Agbomè. In 1787, the Fon King, completely opposed to any European project aimed at organizing trade for the benefit of the Kingdom of Xogbonu (also known as Porto-Novo) and to the detriment of Gléhué, ordered two of his principal officers from Gléhué to attack Porto-Novo. On June 6 and 8, 1787, the troops of Kpengla attacked the beach of Porto-Novo, while 11 French vessels and some Portuguese boats were stranded. The *Danxomènu*, the subjects of Danxomè, took back into captivity 14 French, one Portuguese, and 80 canotiers from the Gold Coast under their authority.

Pierre Gourg, who was then the director of the French Fort of Gléhué, went himself to his Majesty from July 6 to 19, 1787, and managed to negotiate the amount of the ransom after long discussions[39]. During his stay in the capital of Danxomè, Gourg realized that in addition to the Europeans arrested during the first half of June 1787, others had been detained for many years. He wrote on July 17: '' Some Portuguese, eight in number, and two Eng-

---

[39] According to the Englishman Archibald Dalzel (quoted by E. Dunglas, 1957, p. 20), the ransom demanded by Kpengla was estimated at nearly £4,600.

lish also came to see me. Among the Portuguese, there are four who have been in captivity for seven years, and three for three years, and one who was taken at Porto-Novo with the French" (P. Verger, 1968a, p. 216).

Following this aggression, the King of Porto-Novo expressed his grievances to Oyo, who sent a delegation to Agbomè in order to inform Kpengla of his displeasure and ordered him not to attack Xogbonu again. To obtain his clemency, the King of Danxomè proposed to the Yoruba authority to share with him the benefits of his expedition (A. Vido, 2019, p. 78). It is then understandable that, whether under the reign of Agaja or under that of Kpengla, Danxomè did not feel any form of inferiority vis-à-vis the European. These Kings did not hesitate to intern or execute Europeans whom they considered dangerous or in opposition to their interests.

This feeling of inferiority, if we can call it that, was felt by Danxomè towards Oyo, an African state which, at that time, posed as a superpower in the entire Gulf of Benin. For the Fon, it was crucial to avoid any form of confrontation with the Yoruba cavalry, which had sufficient experience carry out raids within Dahomean territory. The Europeans, generally based on the coast and being numerically few, did not pose an immediate threat to Danxomè.

Detainees with White Skin were identified during the reign of Adandozan (1797-1818). Established in Gléhué as part of his commercial activities, the Brazilian Francisco Félix de Souza[40] had serious disagreements with the prince who ascended to the throne of Danxomè under the strong name of Adandozan, probably due to an unsettled debt during a transaction aimed at exchanging slaves for goods. He went to Agbomè to claim the sum due, but the king had him imprisoned for what he considered an affront: '' I would like to know what you have in your head and which gives you so much audacity. As I rather believe that it is the color of your skin that you want to use to face the Idol of the Danhomênou, I will be able to force you to its veneration''. As punishment for Souza, tradition claims that the monarch locked him up and that his guardians immersed him in a large indigo jar, an operation which was repeated several times over several weeks (P. Hazoumé, 1956, p. 28-29; A. L. Araujo, 2007, p. 230-231).

Another White individual was recognized as a prisoner during the reign of Adandozan. It is Innocencio Marques de Santa Anna. According to research by

---

[40] Born in 1754 in Bahia (Salvador) in Brazil, this individual is the descendant of a Portuguese and an Amerindian. Died in Gléhué in 1849, he is the ancestor of all the de Souza that can be identified in Benin and Togo.

the Brazilian historian Ana Lucia Araujo (2014, p. 138), the King of Danxomè sent a diplomatic mission to Bahia, Brazil, which arrived in Salvador in February 1805 aboard the ship *Lepus*. This mission included two *Danxomènu* ambassadors and an interpreter, who was none other than Innocencio Marques de Santa Anna. The latter had been held prisoner for several years in Agbomè, because unlike the English and the French, the Portuguese authorities, through the intermediary of the governor of the Portuguese Fort of Gléhué, were generally not in the habit of paying ransoms to free their compatriots captured at Danxomè.

The absence of an inferiority complex towards Europeans, illustrated by the arrest of European citizens, is also observed during the reign of Gbèhanzin (1890-1894). The Berlin Conference of 1884-1885 led to the establishment of spheres of influence between the major European colonial powers of the time, such as France, Great Britain and Germany. This caused a race to occupy Africa. France wished to establish a colonial empire and sought revenge for the humiliation suffered during the defeat of 1870. To counter the English, who had settled in the east, and the Germans in the west, in what became Togo, she tried to appropriate the Kingdom of Danxomè, in conflict with that of Xogbonu, on which she had already obtained a protectorate.

In 1890, France wished to acquire full control of the cities of Cotonou and Gléhué, already under its occupation, which Kings Glèlè (1858-1889) and Gbèhanzin refused. One day, the French governor Jean Bayol invited the authorities of Cotonou to come and express their complaints, informing them of France's intention to establish itself in a sustainable manner. When the representatives of the King of Danxomè rose up against this, Bayol had them arrested and handed them over to their greatest adversary, King Tofa of Xogbonu, where they underwent inhuman treatment.

In reaction to this, Gbèhanzin gave the order to arrest the Europeans at Gléhué, especially the French. The latter, in chains, headed towards Agbomè. On the way, at Allada[41], they were presented to the king; afterwards, they continued their journey towards Kana until Agbomè where they were presented to the royal court as prisoners of war. From Agbomè, they headed to Zagnanado where they again met the Fon king. The latter ordered one of the prisoners, Alexandre Dorgère, to write a long letter intended for President Sadi Carnot. Gbèhanzin subsequently

---

[41] In this text, we note '' Allada '' with two ''l'' to refer to this region which was under the rule of Danxomè since 1724. On the other hand, when we write '' Alada '' with a single ''l'', we are referring to the independent Kingdom founded by the Aïzo.

granted them freedom and offered them gifts (R. P. Dorgère, 1955, p. 9-16).

As in 1890, the year 1892 was also marked by problems of arrests and White hostages, without any hesitation. Félix Lino de Souza, nephew of *Chacha* Julião de Souza, as well as his friend Félix Arnold, son of an English trading captain, were caught in the act of espionage near the forts and fortified houses of Xogbonu. This operation was carried out on behalf of Danxomè. They were apprehended on April 29, 1892, and each of them was incarcerated in a fort. Gbèhanzin's reaction was not long. He also arrested three French merchants. France, through Colonel Dodds, demanded the release of the hostages and asked the Fon king to withdraw his troops from the regions of Cotonou, Zogbo, and Dogba, which were under the control of his warriors. For purely strategic reasons, Gbèhanzin agreed to release the French detainees (J. A. Djivo, vol. 1, 2013, p. 352-353).

Narratives from the late 19th century describing the clashes between the troops of Danxomè and the French invader, it is difficult to find references to a feeling of inferiority or to a fear felt by an African warrior on the battlefield. On the contrary, the victors, although they were imbued with prejudice towards the Black people, described the bravery of these women and men who sacrificed their lives to preserve the territorial boundaries of Danxomè and especially its greatness, its fame. For example, in a telegram offering information about the fight of October 4, 1892, the following can be read:

> After three hours of fierce fighting, the Dahomeyans were put into complete rout. They fled to the north, leaving a considerable number of corpses and many rapid-fire weapons of the German system (...) The Dahomaeans showed great bravery and an incredible strength of resistance. Amazons were killed ten meters from the square (Fr. Desplantes, 1894, p. 91-93).

It is well established that on January 26, 1894, around 6: 30 a.m., Gbèhanzin, beaten by the French expeditionary force, presented his surrender to Dodds. However, what is much less known is that the king hesitated to extend his hand to the superior officer. It was only after having received the advice of some princes close to him that he ended up doing so (P. Falcon, 1954, p. 18) [42]. What could be the reasons for Gbèhanzin's attitude? Was it the fear of greeting a winner perceived as superior? Was this attitude the reflection of a superstition maintained by the monarch?

---

[42] According to the Beninese historian Luc Garcia (1988, p. 249), '' The meeting with General Dodds was moving. He congratulated him and wanted to shake his hand : Béhanzin refused ''.

To the questions raised, we provide an answer that relies on the sacred character of the king. According to Montserrat Palau Marti (1960, p. 134), in the Kingdom of Danxomè: ''The person of the king is sacred and everything that emanates from it must receive treatment accordingly ''. That is why his subjects, whether they were ordinary citizens, princes, princesses, eminent dignitaries, friends or others, did not fail to bow down before him, covering themselves in dust, in an attitude of absolute submission.

Gbèhanzin, aware that Dodds was not a King like him, did not see him as a person worthy of touching his skin, let alone shaking his hand. The prestigious posture of the Fon monarch, upon his return to Agbomè after a relatively prolonged period in the maquis[43], shows that he still considered himself as King and that by virtue of this quality, he could dialogue with the highest authority in France on an

---

[43] The posture of the King also manifests itself through the quality of his clothing and the dazzling health he displayed upon his return to Agbomè. Regarding the first aspect mentioned, Commander Boutin (quoted by L. Garcia, 1988, p. 249) reported that the King had arrived at the place of his surrender : '' wearing a silk bonnet of Dahomean shape, dressed in a rich loincloth ''. For the second aspect, it should be noted that Gbèhanzin presented himself before Dodds '' in good physical and moral condition, while he declared him sick, eaten away by an infection of the bladder which would have prevented him from walking '' (L. Garcia, 1988, p. 249).

equal footing[44], rather than addressing a senior officer who was, to a lesser extent, the equivalent of his younger brother Goutchili, the future Agoli-Agbo (1894-1900), who was then general in chief of the army of Danxomè.

From what has been stated, it can be concluded that the perception of Africans, in particular that of the inhabitants of Danxomè, towards Europeans, was completely devoid of any feeling of inferiority related to the difference in skin color. The *Danxomènu*, as part of their interests, always strove to take advantage of their relations with the White Man still called *Yovo* in the Fon language, without ever lowering their gaze, which could have been interpreted as a sign of submission or abdication. This feeling was also perceptible towards the mixed-race people, often present in the Kingdom as slaves or wives. Others, considered traitors by the royal court, could be sentenced to life imprisonment in the prisons of Agbomè.

In 1724, while he was held captive at Agbomè, Bullfinch Lamb (cited by G. Smith, vol. 2, 1751, p. 110-111) had the opportunity to observe the interest that *Dada* Agaja showed in moving frequently with a

---

[44] *Dada* Gbèhanzin exiled with the hope of meeting in France the president Sadi Carnot. He believed he could discuss issues related to his Kingdom (B. Adjou-Moumouni, 2017, p. 103).

document containing Christian prayers: '' He likes very much to look into a book, and he usually carries in his pocket a Latin book of prayers (…) and every time he wants to refuse any grace asked of him, he leafs through this book with great attention, as if he heard something about it. He also likes a lot to be greyed on paper ''. According to the observation made by the English, it is possible to indicate that the Fon King had a great interest in reading and writing, activities to which he devoted himself with the help of his Portuguese half-breed slave (I. A. Akinjogbin, 2019, p. 112). However, who was this slave? According to Guillaume Snelgrave (2008, p. 89), he was captured during the conquest of Alada and transferred to Agbomè. As regards Bullfinch Lamb (cited by G. Smith, vol. 2, 1751, p. 95-96), it was acquired by Agaja des Popo (the Hula or Xwla), for an amount of 500 pounds sterling. His main role was '' tailor (…) he has nothing to do but to mend, every two or three months, the clothes of Her Majesty''. According to Lamb's account, the half-caste owned two dwellings in Agbomè, slaves as well as a large number of wives, including an albino.

The advantageous position of the Portuguese half-caste in Agbomè was in no way related to the lighter hue of his skin, which thus brought him closer to the Whites. As a general rule, the Kings of Danxomè, when they identified exceptional talent among individuals captured and sent to Agbomè, had the possibility to put them at their service immediately, while ensuring that they could exercise their profession in complete tranquility. To this end, the Kings, true patrons, could offer these newly arrived scholars wives, lands, and other resources necessary to facilitate their integration into the Kingdom.

The history of Danxomè indicates that the royal residences of Agbomè sheltered mixed-race wives, notably Sophie and Sally, during the reigns of Kpengla, Agonglo (1789-1797) and Adandozan. In 1787, Kpengla welcomed a woman named Sophie Mutatum into his home. Daughter of an agent of the English Fort[45] of Gléhué and a *Danxomènu*, Avléssi Mèdélè, she was born around 1755 and was the wife of Joseph Ollivier de Montaguère, who was in charge of the French Fort. This mixed-race woman had two sons with the Frenchman: Nicolas and Jean-Baptiste Ollivier de Montaguère. According to the available documentation on this subject, two explanations justify Sophie's presence at the royal court.

The first is reported to us by Archibald Dalzel (1793, p. 208-210). After having received a large batch of

---

[45] According to Edna G. Bay (1998, p. 167), Sophie's father was of Dutch origin. On the other hand, Paul Hazoumé (1956, p. 31) argues that he was rather of Portuguese nationality. For his part, Clover Jebsen Afokpa (2002, p. 72) claims that he held French nationality.

coral necklaces from Marseille, the manager of the French Fort gave some of them of average quality to Kpengla. To sell the better quality necklaces, he turned to Madame Paussie, a prosperous merchant established in Gléhué, who managed without too much difficulty to deliver them to the men of the King of Oyo, who came to Kana to receive the annual tribute. By comparing the pearls delivered with the tribute to those acquired by his emissaries, the supreme authority of Oyo was deeply shocked and addressed harsh remonstrations to his vassal Kpengla. Humiliated, the Fon king immediately undertook an investigation which allowed identifying the perpetrators of this diplomatic incident. In disagreement with the monarch of Danxomè, Ollivier de Montaguère decided to leave his position in favor of his compatriot Pierre Gourg. Before returning to his country, he entrusted his wife to King Kpengla with the aim of obtaining from him Gourg's return to France.

Christine Henry (2008, p. 107) presents the second version which explains Sophie's presence in Agbomè. According to his research, Joseph Ollivier de Montaguère, before returning to France to treat a disease from which he was suffering, had confided his wife to King Kpengla. Among the two versions, one thing is certain: the mixed-race was indeed entrusted to Kpengla. Joseph Ollivier de Montaguère never returned to Danxomè. Sophie then stayed at the royal court where she had the privilege of sharing the King's intimacy. She even gave him a son named Agbakossi[46]. Upon Kpengla's death, Sophie married King Agonglo, son and successor of Kpengla. They had a son named Ahokpè.

Upon the death of Agonglo in 1797, Sophie Mutatum married Adandozan. They had a son named Houégbèlo. In addition to Sophie, Adandozan married a mixed-race woman named Sally. She was the daughter of Lionel Abson, governor of the English Fort of Gléhué from 1770 to 1803. Married to an African, this European had four children: three boys and a girl. It was around the age of 20 that Sally became the wife of King Adandozan (J. M. D. McLeod, 1820, p. 85; B. Obichere, 1978, p. 16).

A half-breed, in the history of Danxomè, was accused of ingratitude and treason by Glèlè, which led to his imprisonment, where he lost his life in appalling conditions. His name is Julião Félix de Souza. Son of the Brazilian Francisco Félix de Souza, also known as *Chacha* I, he was educated according to Portuguese principles and acquired a good level of book knowledge, while mastering *fongbé* and

---

[46] This young man, following the death of King Kpengla in 1789, was raised in Gléhué by his half-brother Nicolas Ollivier de Montaguère, also known as Oliveira. Agbakossi resided in the maritime province of Danxomè and was buried there (J. C. Alladayè, 2003, p. 56).

guingbé. Upon the death of Francisco Félix de Souza, known as Chicou (1824-1880), the *Chacha* III, Glèlè designated him as his successor. The King protected him and encouraged him in his efforts, delighted to see many boats anchored in the harbor of Gléhué and satisfied with the resulting prosperity.

Benefiting from the King's trust, Julião de Souza took advantage of this situation to have the maritime province of Danxomè placed under the protection of Portugal. Using the influence he had on Glèlè, he managed to convince him to accept a convention that would establish Gléhué as a Portuguese protectorate. When the European officer sent by the government of São Tomé and Principe arrived with documents ready to be signed, he accompanied him to Agbomè and acted as interpreter. Unable to find a literal translation for the term '' protectorate '', he used the expression '' reciprocal friendship''. This appealed to King Glèlè who signed the document. In 1885, he even proposed sending an embassy to Portugal.

However, two years later, the situation became complex. A member of the royal entourage suggested to the King that Julião de Souza had ceded Gléhué to Portugal, signifying that this land no longer belonged to him. In June 1887, the King invited *Chacha* IV to go to the capital for urgent business. It was a ploy to trap Julião, who had no idea what was going on. Upon his arrival in Agbomè, he was forced to explain himself and rejected all the accusations against him. Glèlè then decided to submit him to a test dictated by a deity, who declared his guilt. He was immediately chained, beaten and imprisoned. The King then summoned all the children of Julião. He made them believe that their father was calling them one by one. When questioned, those deemed complicit in Julião's actions were sent to prison. After the children, it was the turn of the parents and close friends of the *Chacha*. Once the investigation was completed, the culprits were gathered in a hut transformed into a pyre and perished in the flames.

Paulin, one of the sons of Julião Félix de Souza, aged 17 years, tried to escape, but he was caught and imprisoned. After several years of incarceration, his older brother, Germano, being in a nearby cell, fearing that he would die without descent, sent him, through the servant assigned to bring them food, a message written in Portuguese with a piece of coal. In this message, he encouraged his younger brother to impregnate the servant named Reynodo. Paulin was beheaded in 1893 by the men of King Gbèhanzin. Nine months later, Reynodo gave birth to François, son of Paulinus.

King Glèlè ordered the destruction of the roof of Julião's house and the confiscation of the property of all the surviving relatives. Upon the announcement of the death of Julião Félix de Souza, his eldest son went to Agbomè to remove his body and give him a burial in Gléhué. He noticed that his father's nose and mouth were filled with sand, on the one hand, and that the body was in a state of advanced decomposition, on the other. He managed to identify her thanks to his gray flannel clothes, the ring he wore on his right hand and the gold dental crown. On 26 December 1887, the Lisbon cabinet renounced the Portuguese protectorate over Gléhué (S. de Souza, 1992, p. 55-57; M. Vido and A. Vido, 2022, p. 154-160).

For the Kings mentioned above, the territories belonging to Danxomè could under no circumstances be transferred to another power, due to their inalienable status, belonging to royal power and, by extension, to all the *Danxomènu* who had to imperatively preserve them, sometimes even at the expense of their life, the ultimate sacrifice. Observing a subject of the Kingdom, whether mixed-race or not, giving up even a small piece of this precious land could only arouse the anger of the monarchs and lead to drastic decisions, which could go as far as measures of physical elimination. For the throne, the individual at fault, whether Black or White, had to become an example to dissuade those who, in their heart of hearts, maintained similar ambitions.

In the first chapter of this study, we indicated that theories concerning the presumed inferiority of Blacks were widely developed and disseminated starting from the 18th century. However, what is less known is that during this period, in France for example, a significant migration of the rural population to the cities was observed. The little people crowded into unsanitary housing. A stench prevailed everywhere. Wastewater was poured from windows directly into the street, which was announced by the famous '' water station''. There was no flushing system, and people relieved themselves wherever they could: in latrines, or most often in more or less discreet corners.

Meanwhile, water was seen as a vector of disease. Dirt, on the other hand, constituted a protective layer against them. At that time, '' being clean '' was limited to a question of appearance: having White and impeccable clothes. The courtiers changed shirts up to five times a day. The people, who could not afford this luxury, were thus laved more frequently than the courtiers. To hide all these smells, he scented himself with stronger and stronger essences. Women, for their part, wore makeup and used musk balls in the mouth to perfume their breath (V. Costes, 2020, p. 10-11).

While some European intellectuals of the 18th and 19th centuries were trying to convince their compatriots of the alleged inferiority of Blacks compared to Whites, others, whether they were travel authors or simple compilers of unpublished stories, often also marked by racist prejudices, did not hesitate however to recognize, sometimes against their own will, in the Black Man significant civilizational values and free from any Western influence. At a time when a lack of personal hygiene was seen as an effective method of fighting disease in Europe, Black People enjoyed washing themselves. The observations of the French doctor Édouard Binet (1900, p. 246) concerning the women and men of the Kingdom of Danxomè reveal that:

> Moreover, the indigenous people are very clean; every day they immerse themselves in water, head to toe, then rub their bodies with palm oil. At the time of childbirth, the woman is assisted by a matrone who gives her the necessary care. If some accident occurs, we call upon the lights of the indigenous doctor. Childbirth can last several days. After birth, the woman is washed with hot water; the child also undergoes washing on all parts of the body.

Before the doctor Binet, Jules Poirier (1896, p. 32), another French author, had noticed the importance that the *Danxomènu* attached to their personal hygiene: '' The use of baths is general; sometimes, the negro washes himself three times a day ''. For the

Africans residing in the south of present-day Benin, personal hygiene was necessarily accompanied by that of clothing: '' Cleanliness care, the use of baths, are in honor. Morning and evening, along the lagoons we see negresses washing their soap, washing their loincloths '' (A. L. d'Albéca, 1895, p. 160). Even in the seventeenth century, in the Aïzo Kingdom of Alada, the practice of daily baths for the care of the body was scrupulously observed: '' Men and women take great care to keep themselves clean, and do not fail to wash evening and morning '' (O. Dapper, 1686, p. 304).

In the 18th century in France, while writers formulated their theories on the superiority of Whites over Blacks, dental hygiene, as we understand it today, was almost absent for the ordinary citizen. It was limited to removing, using any available piece of wood, food residues stuck between the teeth and, perhaps, at times rubbing the teeth with a dry cloth, water being considered harmful to the gums and teeth[47]. In addition, it should be noted that several

---

[47] During the Middle Age, the French, especially those of high society, used to clean their teeth from time to time with a piece of cloth. While the idea of White People's superiority over others was developing, they were probably unaware that the first representation of toothbrushes as we know it today came from China (1498), a region inhabited by non-Whites. It is very likely that they were also not aware that this invention appeared in Europe

people used to eat raw onions for breakfast (J.-P. Hardy and N. Castéran, 2002, p. 13). This certainly contributed to the appearance of breath problems! At the same time, the inhabitants of Lower Benin, to prevent bad breath and maintain the shine of their teeth, resorted daily to vegetable fibers mentioned by the Frenchman Édouard Foà (1895, p. 157) in these terms:

> The country's toothpicks are small pieces of hard wood whose end is mashed until it is softened, forming a kind of brush that we use to rub our teeth in all directions. Black People take great care of their teeth, of which they are proud. They thus clean their mouths several times a day, upon waking up and after meals.

The same author writes that the teeth of the *Danxomènu*: '' are naturally very beautiful (...) well arranged, solid in their alveoli, they are the most beautiful ornament of the face of women" (E. Foà, 1895, p. 103). In 1884, Hugo Zöller (1990, p. 204) spent several weeks in Togo as a reporter for an influential newspaper in the Rhineland. In his account, which covers the regions of Agouè and Grand-Popo, the German author notes the following:

---

much later, during the first half of the 17th century, in Paris (A. Pasquini, 2002, p. 62, 94).

> Black Women give special care to the mainte-
> nance of their short-cut hair and the cleanliness
> of their mouth. They almost always have at
> hand a toothpick, coming from a particular
> wood that serves both as a toothbrush and
> toothpaste: they spend ten times more time on
> dental care than a European.

Apart from physical and oral hygiene, Africans have always attached great importance to the cleanliness of their immediate environment. For them, keeping their house in a healthy state was essential to preserve good health. For example, the ruling class of Danxomè placed particular emphasis on the cleanliness of their apartments. In December 1773, the English traveler-author Robert Norris (1790, p. 141) visited *Dada* Tégbésu (1740-1774) and observed: '' He had a very clean room, in which he slept ''. Nearly a century later, under the reign of Glèlè, a similar observation is made, this time concerning the residence of the heir apparent Ahanhanzo. In 1871, the British naturalist J. Alfred Skertchly (1874, p. 158), who was at Agbomè, provided a description of the interior of the prince's residence in these terms:

> We alighted from our hammock, and, after pro-
> ceeding through several courtyards, arrived at a
> long shed beneath which a row of highly pol-
> ished guns were arranged on a table, while car-
> tridgebelts, powder-horns, and other implements

of warfare decorated the walls. The whole place was beautifully clean and neat; not a stray leaf being visible on the smoothly swept floor. About a dozen guards lazed about, some smoking and others busily engaged sleeping. Beneath the roof, suspended from the rafters, a peculiar machine like a fly-cage attracted my attention. It was made of twigs bent into a hexagonal form, and covered with blue and white cotton yarn in stripes, like those on a water melon. From the lower portion of this cage a square of parchment was hung, illuminated in blue and scarlet, and inscribed with a verse from the Koran. This was a Mohammetan charm against fire.

While the great theorists of the alleged superiority of the White Man over the Black gradually introduced this reflection devoid of solid scientific arguments into the minds of the Europeans, they had undoubtedly omitted to mention that in Paris, in France, in 1880, insalubrity reached its peak and had significant consequences on health (P. Zylberman, 2017, p. 24-25). Simultaneously, in other regions considered uncivilized by the proponents of the hierarchy of the human species, the cleanliness of cities was a priority. During his trip to Agbomè in 1856, Lieutenant Auguste Vallon (t. 3, 1861, p. 337) was able to observe for himself the importance that the *Danxomènu* attached to sanitation. Indeed, during his stopover in Kana, he noticed that the city: '' has nothing remarkable but its admirable situation and its great cleanliness".

From the above, it can be stated that the people of Africa, concerned about their personal, oral and environmental hygiene, did not wait for Europe to impose on them ways of life and techniques to integrate into their daily lives. Concerned about their physical image, they took care of the health of their skin and their smile. Aware of the importance of avoiding diseases related to the insalubrity of their environment, they took care of their living environment, whether it was near or far. Should this qualify us as '' savages '', '' barbarians '' or '' primitives ''? Absolutely not! The theories promoted by some Europeans, which had a considerable impact, failed to recognize the ability of the Black Man to (re)define himself according to his own current needs or interests, without waiting for directives from the other!

When discussing the history of the transatlantic Slave trade, most of the documents available highlight its pre-eminence in the economic activities of African societies. This suggests that, apart from selling his compatriots to the European Slave Traders present on the coasts for this activity, the Black Man excelled in nothing else, thus thanking the European for having freed him from a chronic idleness which led him towards various excesses such as polygamy, alcohol or tobacco. However, if one takes the time to examine the history of Slave Trade objectively, one inevitably finds a fact: this subject must be analyzed on a case-by-case basis. By proceeding in this way, it then becomes possible to qualify the discourse by emphasizing that in certain regions of the African continent, such as Danxomè, the Slave Trade has not been the predominant economic activity.

Indeed, according to the work of the English historian Patrick Manning (1993, p. 165), during the precolonial period, the income generated by the sale of slaves constituted on average 1.5% of the gross domestic product (GDP) of southern Benin today. Similarly, the studies carried out at the end of the 1970s by Werner Peukert (cited by A. Guézo, 2010, p. 88) on the Slave Trade in Danxomè make a valuable contribution to the history of this Kingdom in the 18th century. Based on a statistical analysis covering all social categories, his research showed that the Slave Trade contributed only about 20% to the accumulation of national wealth.

Thus, for the last two authors mentioned, the Slave Trade undoubtedly occupied a significant but not dominant part of the regional economy, which was mainly based on agricultural activities. The book published in 2025, entitled *Les femmes dans l'histoire du Bas-Bénin (XVIIe-XIXe siècles)*, as well as the one titled *L'histoire du riz africain dans le Sud-Bénin*

(XVIIe-XXe siècle): une contribution à l'étude de l'histoire rurale du Bénin, published in 2014, carefully examine the topic that we encourage the reader to delve deeper.

Regarding the links between the Black Man residing in the southern region of present-day Benin and agriculture, it is undeniable that they are appreciated for their true value. For example, as head of the agricultural service, Nicolas Savariau (1906, p. 20) observes the following:

> (The) indigenous farmer has (really) curious (good) habits to study. He leaves his hut at dawn, packs up and smokes his pipe with tranquility, exchanges with his neighbors endless salutes, examines the weather and finally decides to set off. Arrived at the gletas (field), he rests for a few minutes, eats two or three akassa balls and then gets to work. He grabs his hoe, initially spades slowly, then gradually comes to life. After having believed him at first indolent, one is surprised to see him for three or four hours wielding his hoe with tireless activity and surprising dexterity, stopping just occasionally to take a little break or return their salvation to the people who pass by. During the hottest hours of the day, from about 11:00 AM to 2:00 AM, he interrupts his task, has breakfast and sleeps; then he goes back to work until the time when he must leave the gletas to return to the village

before night. The indigenous person working at the Glétas does not spare his pain.

This '' curious'' behavior of the African peasant, which is actually common to all farmers in the world, evokes certain similarities with other authors. Georges Borelli (quoted by J.-R. Chandon de Briailles, 1902, p. 21) points out in this regard that:

> Nothing can give a more exact idea of Dahomey life than that of our small villages in France; was it not the color of the inhabitants, it would be to err there. The cottages are ours, with their walls of clay and thatched roofs, arranged in no order around a large square shaded by beautiful trees, under which the old and the chiefs walk or palate while smoking the pipe; the young people cultivate the fields nearby; the old women spin cotton on the threshold of their cottages with the cattail of our grandmother.

For many years, it has been common to hear, teachers and African compatriots affirm that democracy has never concerned the Black Man. However, whenever one asks them to provide scientific evidence to support such a claim, they found it very difficult to do so. In the best case, they argued that it was contact with the West that led to the introduction and spread of democratic practices. For Africans who adopt this perspective, we recommend that they read with great interest the doctoral thesis of Patrick

Joël Adjivèssodé which deals with *La question des droits de la personne humaine en Afrique subsaharienne précoloniale: le cas du Danxomɛ des origines à l'occupation française.*

Defended in 2015 at the University of Abomey-Calavi, this thesis indicates that the current events on the African continent after independence, marked by the confiscation of freedoms, coups d'État and the establishment of extraordinary regimes, could have made believe that pre-colonial Africa had never known a democratic culture or respect for human rights. Yet, African civilizations had established democratic systems and displayed respect for human dignity in accordance with their values and traditions. For the Beninese historian, the error lies in trying to analyze these two values according to pre-established models, valid for other societies, especially European ones. It is wrong to consciously or unconsciously lose sight of the fact that democracy and human rights are in reality the fruit of a culture, of a civilization, and ultimately, concepts with variable geometry. According to Patrick Joël Adjivèssodé, it is indisputable that African traditions were the bearers of several values compatible with human rights. This is what he proved by taking the example of the Kingdom of Danxomè.

In the Kingdom of Danxomè, because of the devotion of his subjects and the immense scope of his prerogatives, the King was frequently considered a tyrant ruling by arbitrary power and enjoying great impunity. However, in truth, counterbalancing mechanisms were present within the power, bringing balance to royal authority. In addition to custom, which represents the supreme and sacred norm, serving as the first bulwark against a capricious administration of power, the social body and the institutions of control of power represented instances with which the King had to cooperate, at the risk of compromising his throne (P. J. Adjivèssodé, 2016, p. 41-55).

It is also good to know that, by his birth, the King was supposed to have a double origin combining nobility and roture. These observations are made by Camille Piétri (1890, p. 387) who declares: '' A King in Dahomey is never the son of his father and of a woman of Dahomean race. He must be the son of a slave of another race, because the law of the land says that a son wastes the good of his fathers, while a stranger keeps it ''. According to Jérôme C. Alladayè (2008, p. 49), this measure was aimed at promoting social integration and cohesion as well as ensuring strict management of public affairs. Social integration and cohesion also included the descendants of slaves.

When a child, whether a daughter or a son of a slave, came into the world on the soil of Danxomè, he automatically acquired the right to the soil, thus becoming a citizen of Danxomè or *Danxomènu*. Camille-N. Piétri (1890, p. 387) notes on this subject: '' The position of the son of a slave is in no way dishonorable, for every individual born in the land of Dahomey is free and cannot be sold ''. For the rulers, this right was a way to limit the formation of a community of slaves possessing their own language and culture, while perceiving themselves as strangers to the Kingdom. This inhibited any tendency to withdraw into identity and also hindered the emergence of a hybrid civilization (P. J. Adjivèssodé, 2015, p. 237). While the Danxomè applied *jus soli* at the latest since the beginning of the 18th century, it was necessary to wait until 1868 for the 14th amendment of the US constitution to grant nationality at birth on the basis of *jus soli*. This means that all children born on the soil of the United States of America acquired US citizenship without it being necessary to distinguish according to the status of their parents[48].

From what has just been expressed, it is clear that the Danxomè mobilized the necessary resources to establish a society in which each individual, whether no-

---

[48] Cf. https://www.letemps.ch/monde/droit-sol-americain-tirs-croises-republicains?srsltid=AfmBOopTvca32WCFg9UEWt-nEqQY-rpF6AWQhi-KLDhHldsAE3Ms-DcO. Visited on February 2, 2026 at 1 hour 3 minutes.

ble or ordinary, felt integrated and could participate in its development in all areas. In doing so, the people and leaders reached this goal without feeling inferiority towards other human groups, thus highlighting the importance of citizenship and cultural diversity. This relatively unknown aspect of the history of the Fon leads us to affirm that: '' there is nothing new under the sun '' (Ecclesiastes 1: 9). We must remember that the White Man has not taught everything to the Black World!

During the period preceding colonization, within the societies of Atakora, located in the north-west of present-day Benin, democracy manifested itself at the base by an individual autonomy which was radically different from individualism. Indeed, the individual was not subject to any control exercised by anyone and enjoyed great freedom of initiative in his daily life (E. Tiando, 1978, pp. 126-128). Moreover, there was no form of social differentiation between individuals, whether by birth or by occupation; rights and obligations were the same for all, only age and sex determining the status of each (J. Lombard, 1967, p. 22-23).

As for the families, they were all autonomous and free, while being united with other families belonging to the same lineage. Within lineages and clans (or groups of lineages), the relations between the heads of families participating in the council of elders were based on egalitarian foundations. Everyone, including the religious leader who headed this council, enjoyed an equal audience and decisions were generally made by consensus (C. T. M. Kounkouaga, 2003, p. 47-48).

Roger N'Tia (1993, p. 115-117) provides details regarding the identification of socio-cultural groups that have actually practiced democracy in Atakora. According to this Beninese historian, among them are Biyobè (or Soruba), Kabyè, Lokpa, Bialbè (or Berba), Bèbèlibè (or Niendé), Natemaa, Bètammaribè, as well as Waaba-Tangamba-Daataba group. All these communities established in the Atakora massif were described by the French colonizer and by researchers as anarchic societies, due to the absence of a centralized political system. However, they failed to recognize that the previously mentioned human groups had long since chosen to adopt a political system based on strict respect for customs and elders. Moreover, initiation, from which it was impossible to escape without consequences in most of these societies, defined the prerogatives and duties of individuals. These societies were in reality deeply democratic and not societies without order where the individual was left to himself and his frivolities.

Marriage without the consent of the girl is a subject that has been debated at length by human rights specialists, to the point where one might think that before colonization, it was the norm in Africa. The girl was often given by her parents to a man whom she did not truly love; the parents being judged as the only ones capable of determining what was beneficial for her in matters of matrimonial alliances. However, by taking the time to study our history, that of Africa, we realize one essential thing: it is relevant to evaluate the facts studied on a case-by-case basis. Indeed, it is appropriate to nuance our studies and our discourses concerning our history, because a widely accepted and recognized reality in one community could differ elsewhere, even within the same family. In the Kingdom of Danxomè, for example, it was sometimes required that a father, to consent to the marriage of his daughter, ask for his opinion. It is depending on the response provided by the girl that marriage could be established or not. During the second half of the 18th century, an anonymous author (1778, p. 16) had noted the following:

> Men of all ages may want to make their wives a young girl (...) when they like it. They compliment it on the father. If he agrees, he sends for his daughter and asks her if she wants to take him for her man. If without way she says that yes, it is over. The future has 5 gallines of cowry, a bottle of brandy. And it is only a question of it when the daughter is married, so the future husband is warned about it (...) He gives his fu-

ture 15 to 20 daggers and 5 handkerchiefs according to his fortune.

Africa, throughout its long and rich history, has seen the emergence of eminent intellectuals trained on the continent. For example, in the 15th and 16th centuries, Timbuktu was the main intellectual and religious centre of the western Sudan. This city attracted thousands of students from all over Sudan. As a terminus of the trans-Saharan caravans and a receptacle of ideas and goods from the Mediterranean regions, it has reached an unprecedented level of civilization and culture in the West African space. His culture was fundamentally characterized by the primacy of the spirit over all things, a spirit in search of God and human wisdom.

A powerful and respected class of intellectuals from all communities played a key role in educating the people by example, shining the torch of the spirit. The term intelligentsia, which in the 19th century referred to the class of Russian intellectuals engaged in the quest for reform of their society, is inappropriate to describe the doctors of Timbuktu who were respectful of the established order. The latter formed a class conscious of its role as a special category in society. At that time, Timbuktu was a cosmopolitan city where all the recognized sociolinguistic communities in Sudan coexisted without the racism that has emerged over the past centuries. Individuals were judged according to their birth, piety or knowledge. Moreover, all the literati were aware of belonging to a specific category, that of intelligence, whose mission was to instruct (S. M. Cissoko, 1969, p. 48, 55).

Conclusion

In conclusion, it becomes evident that a multitude of cultural values have shaped African societies as autonomous entities, entirely free from any sense of inferiority towards the West. Numerous examples from the southern, central, western, and northern regions of the continent clearly demonstrate an ability to evolve with exceptional intelligence, independent of external influences, by forming remarkable societies structured into Empires, Kingdoms, Chiefdoms, and decentralized communities. The historical illustrations of this sovereign identity are limitless and prolific. Thus, it remains difficult to formulate a definitive conclusion when evoking what the cradle of humanity represented at any specific point in its history. Nevertheless, it is essential to propose this reflection, despite the vast fields of research that remain to be explored!

This study has highlighted that it is undeniable that the Black Man, at no time, we repeat it, at no time, was cursed and is cursed. All the biblical and pseudo-scientific arguments aimed at justifying it have been dismantled! In fact, it was necessary for the Arab-Muslim and European populations to defend reasons of this kind in order to justify enslaving a part of humanity, with the aim of supporting their respective economies, and exploiting the rich lands of Africa, both in agricultural products and mineral resources. For the Europeans, for example, it would have been morally unacceptable to pillage this rich continent without having first advanced civilising arguments such as: '' Black People are barbarians '', '' African People are savages'', '' African People are ferocious beasts'', '' Blacks are primitives '', ''Blacks practice fetishism'', ''Blacks are lazy'', '' Blacks have no souls, they don't know God'', ''We must bring them God and civilization'', ''We must save their souls from eternal condemnation, from the flames of hell '', ''Black People have no history, we must bring them a bit of humanity '', etc. The list is endless!

For all these morally unsustainable and scientifically unjustifiable reasons, Europe has, following the Berlin Conference, decided to conquer mother earth. The Germans, English, Belgians, Spanish, French, Italians and others, galvanized by racial stereotypes placing them above others, have invaded Africa, causing the deaths of women, children and men with impunity. They annihilated or pillaged cultural assets that today enrich their museums. More than anything, the plundering of Africa has led to a disorganization of many political institutions. European colonizers deliberately weakened the established authorities by favouring new leaders, many of whom came from princes traditionally not allowed to rise to power, commoners or freed former slaves. The establishment of this mode of power management violated the sacred nature of ancestral authority.

In its enterprise of '' civilization '', Europe has decided to subject chiefs to military recruitment as well as forced labor as part of a quota policy. This situation naturally led the Africans, oppressed but always worthy, to rise up, revolts which were cruelly repressed (as evidenced by the examples of Kaba, the Saxwè and the Holli of present-day Benin). The leaders considered as accomplices of these revolts were arrested, imprisoned and sometimes exiled far from their ancestors' lands, where some lost their lives in extreme poverty. In his project '' civiliser '', the White Man has stripped the legitimate holder of power for the benefit of a new leader deemed docile, malleable and ready to defend the interests of the foreigner.

In his quest to build a '' civilization'' in Africa, the White Man altered the unity of the territorial framework within which societies evolved. For example, the power centers in the Hausa region such as Zinder or Maradi, currently in Niger, which fell under French authority, were thus separated from their equivalents in Nigeria, now integrated into the British colonial empire. In order to better unbalance a freshly colonized Africa, it was decided to establish structures aimed at training local leaders. In this context, the school aimed primarily at creating an elite capable of facilitating the administration of colonized territories, rather than empowering Africans to manage the future of their respective countries.

The Western educational institution thus contributed to establishing a system of wealth extraction within the framework of a vast colonial empire, whose economic exploitation required local intermediaries adhering to ideologies from abroad. Moreover, the Western school has gradually changed the mentality of the Black Man by transmitting new values to him, those of the colonizing West! African leaders have gradually detached themselves from their societies of origin, sometimes considering them as retrograde, obsolete and uninnovative! For the colonized of French West Africa, their ancestors were now identified as the Gauls! Thus, down to *Dada* Gbèhanzin!

Concerned by the idea of destabilizing the Blacks in order to appropriate their property, the White colonizer engaged in a certain '' modernization '' of agricultural practices, mainly aimed at exporting the necessary raw materials. The main cultures introduced into African societies in this perspective have led to complications. Among these, it can be noted that the forced migration of workers from areas poorly adapted to cash crop farming to more favorable regions has upset the structures of rural societies. Moreover, the fall in prices of these crops, caused by the continuous deterioration of exchange conditions, has prevented the majority of farmers from benefiting from their efforts. This has led to a worsening of poverty, with repercussions such as food insecurity, malnutrition-related diseases and changes in eating habits, thus exacerbating dependence on the international market[49].

Today more than ever, Africans are fully aware of a reality: European colonization has really brought nothing beneficial! Can anything imposed by force, without the consent of the other, have positive effects? Does raping a woman and making her pregnant, thus offering her the opportunity to perpetuate a lineage and humanity, make the rapist a benefactor? In no case! Should Africans remember these

---

[49] All the concepts concerning the disorganization of Africa by colonizing Europe come from the article written by the Beninese geographer John O. Igué, published in 2009, and entitled *Le rôle de la colonisation dans l'« immobilisme » des sociétés africaines.* Read also Nouréïni Tidjani-Serpos (1975, p. 102-106).

painful episodes of their history, as if they were stirring the knife in the wound? Absolutely! And why? Simply to identify those who have largely contributed to the underdevelopment of their continent! They must resolutely engage in a process of personal development so as to no longer be subjected to the domination of those who previously exercised control over them! It is essential for Africans to work on themselves to recognize their strengths as well as their weaknesses, in order to prevent this from happening again!

Above all, it is crucial to realize that long before the arrival of the European colonizers, Africa had its own history, its own conflicts, as well as methods to resolve them, various societies, women and men striving tirelessly to protect their achievements in dignity, and economic practices, food, political, religious, cultural, etc., which were specific to each region of the cradle of humanity. By giving, Africans have played an essential role in the development of the rest of the world in every conceivable field. In receiving, they integrated what came from elsewhere while seeking to adapt it to their context for their well-being.

Today more than ever, Africans who have grown up and studied in primary, secondary, and university educational institutions on the continent, possess a way of thinking distinct from that of their elders who, them, lived and suffered colonization or the beginnings of neocolonialism. For these Africans of Africa, who have been trained by Black teachers, Black educators, Black tutors, and who are inspired by Black achievements, Black heroes, and other Black figures, they have already become aware that the most essential element to preserve to promote development in all fields is the way of thinking. This mentality allows them to understand without much difficulty that Whites are in reality only individuals like themselves. No more!

Nowadays, Africans are becoming aware that the West is not really this idyllic world that we have always wanted to present; while the United States of America is actively engaged in the repatriation of thousands of illegal immigrants outside its territory, and that they carry out military attacks against countries they consider to be ruled by dictators, as evidenced by the extradition of Venezuelan president Nicolas Maduro to USA, this is not only aimed at regulating massive immigration to their country or even improving the global situation. In reality, it is mainly to guarantee the exploitation of Venezuela's oil resources and to divert public attention, both nationally and internationally, from a palpable reality: the gradual decline of U.S. Status as the world's leading economic power, now threatened by China[50]. Although many Africans continue to dream of going there by all means, a significant part of the observant, silent, and industrious youth[51] is built in pain, sorrow, joy, and hope on the continent of their ancestors.

---

[50] In an article published on January 8, 2026, Rémy Larquetoux, journalist for *Business Cool*, an online site, presents the ranking of countries according to their GDP for the year 2025. The United States of America ranks first with a GDP of USD 30.507 billion, followed by China in second place with USD 19.231 billion. After China, we find Germany (USD 4,744 billion), India (USD 4,187 billion), Japan (USD 4,186 billion), the United Kingdom (USD 3,839 billion), France (USD 3,211 billion), Italy (USD 2,422 billion), Canada (USD 2,225 billion) and finally Brazil (USD 2,126 billion). Cf. https://business-cool.com/decryptage/analyse/classement-puissances-mondiales/. Visited on 25 January 2026 at 8 hours 58 minutes. However, when GDP is presented in purchasing power parity (PPP), according to estimates by the International Monetary Fund (IMF), China's GDP ranks first since 2014. See https://major-prepa.com/geopolitique/ perspec-tives-geoeconomoques-chine/. Accessed 25 January 2026 at 9 : 17 AM.

[51] Africa is currently the youngest continent on the planet, with more than 60% of its population under 25 years old. By 2050, this demographic potential will peak, reaching more than 830 million young people, representing more than a quarter of the world's population. This pool of young talents offers an unprecedented opportunity to stimulate the economy, foster innovation and tackle sustainable development issues. Cf. https://zawadi-initiatives.org/les-3-raisons-qui-font-de-la-jeunesse-africaine-latout-majeur-du-developpement-africain/. Visited 25 January 2026 at 13 hours 17 minutes.

Currently, young Africans are following with divided interest the relations between the United States of America and Europe. Until recently, these two entities were seen as political and economic partners, working closely together to provide both positive and negative assessments to nations and world leaders on governance and economic management. However, it now appears that these two parties are preparing to distance themselves on various fronts. In a 33-page document, published in November 2025, which presents the White House's strategy on major international issues, only 2.5 pages were attributed to Europe, with an alarming tone: '' Migration policies are transforming the continent. If this trend continues, he will be unrecognizable within 20 years or perhaps less ''. This observation generates a clear will: '' Our objective should be to help Europe correct its current trajectory ''.

According to David Thomson, a French journalist who is interested in the Make America Great Again[52] movement, this rectification involves increasing interference in European affairs: '' What Donald Trump's White House and this new right wants to do is to replace the current European elites with whom they believe they cannot work, the elites they

---

[52] '' Make America Great Again '' is an electoral slogan used by political figures in the United States of America.

describe as liberal, left and right alike, with a counter-European elite, nationalist, populist, who is aligned with their agenda[53] ''.

Specifically, french President Emmanuel Macron, due to his refusal to join the Peace Council for Gaza, received an almost immediate response from US President Donald Trump, who stated: '' No one wants its membership. But he will do it if a 200% tax is imposed on French wine and champagne. In reality, everyone doesn't care, whether he adheres or not[54] ''. From the point of view of Africa, in particular the territories that suffered French colonialism, this declaration resonates for many as a humiliating defeat, a slap inflicted on someone who had previously seemed powerful, invincible and feared. Masks fall, reality sometimes tastes bitter, but it's reality. France, a former colonial power, can be ridiculed in the eyes of everyone without even being able to react appropriately. In the eyes of many Africans, it is slowly eroding, its influence on the world, particularly in Africa, has undeniably diminished.

---

[53]   Cf.   https://www.franceinfo.fr/monde/usa/presidentielle/donald-trump/donald-trump-et-la-politique-de-l-humiliation-contre-l-europe_7752118.html. Visited on 25 January 2026 at 9 hours 54 minutes.

[54] Cf. https://www.courrierinternational.com/article/vu-de-chine-apres-l-humiliation-publique-de-macron-par-trump-l-europe-doit-se-reveiller_239645. Visited 25 January 2026 at 10 hours 22 minutes.

Nowadays, the Western powers present themselves as giants with feet of clay. Engaged in a military operation[55] against Iran since February 28, 2026, the United States of America and Israel are having difficulty imposing themselves on the Islamic republic, which does not hesitate to use drones and ballistic missiles not only against Israel, but also against the American military bases located in Jordan, Kuwait, Bahrain, Qatar, Iraq, Saudi Arabia and the United Arab Emirates. Meanwhile, Africa patiently weaves its connections.

Thanks to the immeasurable richness of its cultural heritage, it, which is by no means under a curse, has found its place and has brilliantly established itself in the global film industry through remarkable works such as *Black Panther* (2018), *Black Panther: Wakanda Forever* (2022) and *The Woman King* (2022). To talk only about the first work, this one was directed by the Afro-American Ryan Kyle Coogler and met with phenomenal success at the world box office. It generated $708 million in worldwide revenues, without having yet been broadcast in China or Japan, according to *Box-office mojo*. It is an impressive performance, because until recently, U.S. films featuring Black heroes were not very

---

[55] Initially planned to extend over a few days, this operation has already exceeded one month.

successful outside the United States of America. In France, the film held first place at the box office for some time, totaling 1.7 million admissions in just 12 days, according to *JP Box-office*[56].

At a time when the United States of America is gradually ceding its place to China in terms of the world's leading economic power, and when Europe is struggling to gain respect from the United States, rapidly losing its influence on the Black Continent, Africa, as for it, attracts the attention of the world. Increasingly, there is a significant return of Afro-descendants to their homeland. Many of them, through DNA tests, manage to find, even in an approximate way, the regions of Africa where they are from. Several of them, back in Africa, do not hesitate to take African nationalities, seeking to show the rest of the world that they come from a specific place on the Black Continent.

Today, Afro-descendants feel a real desire to rediscover their roots thanks to the YouTuber IShow-Speed, whose real name is Darren Jason Watkins Jr., one of the most prominent content creators in the world. This 21-year-old Afro-American, who has 50

---

[56] Cf. https://www.bfmtv.com/economie/entreprises/culture-loisirs/pourquoi-black-panther-cartonne-au-box-office_AN-201802270181.html. Visited on 25 January 2025 at 18 hours 11 minutes.

millions subscribers on YouTube, 45 millions on Instagram, and 47 millions on TikTok[57], traveled across the African continent and ignited social networks with his live videos, highlighting that the continent is '' full of surprises[58] ''. This streamer, whose manifest ambition is to '' show the world what Africa is[59] '', has already visited various African countries, notably Benin, while keeping his camera on constantly, thus allowing the Americans to discover a continent far from the clichés of poverty and misery that have long dominated[60].

A large number of Africans who have left their country for an adventure in the West for several years have had the opportunity to undergo training in various fields and have been able to acquire international experience. For many reasons, ranging from

---

[57] Cf. https://www.lemonde.fr/afrique/article/2026/01/24/l-afrique-n-est-pas-comme-je-le-pensais-la-tournee-fren.europa.eu-de-l-influenceur-americain-ishowspeed_6663916_3212.html. Visited on 25 January 2026 at 13 hours 26 minutes.

[58] Cf. https://www.bbc.com/afrique/articles/ce3ezq4e2g7o. Visited on 25 January 2026 at 12 hours 3 minutes.

[59] Cf. https://www.lemonde.fr/afrique/article/2026/01/24/l-afrique-n-est-pas-comme-je-le-pensais-la-tournee-fren.europa.eu-de-l-influenceur-americain-ishowspeed_6663916_3212.html. Visited on 25 January 2026 at 13 : 40.

[60] Cf. https://www.rtl.fr/culture/medias-people/une-afrique-loin-des-stereotypes-comment-le-streameur-ishowspeed-a-ouvert-les-yeux-de-millions-d-internautes-7900591037. Visited on 25 January 2026 at 12 hours 2 minutes.

the rise of the far right in their host countries to new opportunities in Africa, a growing number of them are less and less hesitant to return, while striving to build a future.

While the United States of America is considering appropriating, in a peaceful or coercive manner, Greenland, a territory belonging to the Kingdom of Denmark, without the member countries of the European Union reacting significantly, the Africans of the 21st century, through their history, still remember the greatness of their pre-colonial societies; a greatness that fuels more than ever their consciousness, making them proud, worthy and ready to reclaim the place long taken from them. This place, marked by an inclusive and unprecedented development, thanks to indisputable human, material, natural and spiritual resources, Africa gradually takes it back through the force of work... in 10 years, 30 years, 100 years, 1000 years, it will have completely recovered its place. What do 50 years or 3000 years represent for humanity which counts millions of them? In fact, not much.

Africa, known for its dynamic population, does not define itself as a continent in distress imploring the assistance of others. Cradle of humanity, it does not represent this land pushed into a cry of despair, as it struggles to assert itself. Ignoring the prejudices that

seek to devalue her, not imploring mercy from anyone, she makes significant progress and reinvents
herself proactively. Without a shadow of a doubt,
she decided, as she always did, to make a contribution to the management of the world, whatever the
field, and it is crucial to integrate it into our consid-
erations!

Bibliographical references

Books

ADIKO Assoi and CLÉRICI André, 1963, *Histoire des peuples noirs*, Abidjan, Ceda, 192 p.

ADJOU-MOMOUNI Basile, 2017, *Dogbagri Kokpon. Premier pas d'un roi vers le bout de la terre*, Cotonou, Les Éditions Plurielles, 116 p.

AFOKPA C. J., 2002, *Daxome retold: collective memory and the Historical Museum of Abomey*, Ann Arbor, MI, UMI Dissertation Services, 336 p.

AKINJOGBIN Isaac Adeagbo, 2019, *Le Dahomey dans les relations internationales au XVIIIe siècle*, Sarrebruck, Éditions Universitaires Européennes, translated from English by Anselme Guézo, 233 p.

ALLADAYÈ Jérôme C., 2008, *Fresques Danxoméennes*, Cotonou, Les Éditions du Flamboyant, 120 p.

ALLADAYÈ Jérôme Comlan, 2003, *Le catholicisme au pays du vodun*, Cotonou, Les Éditions du Flamboyant, 459 p.

ANONYME, 1778, *Mémoire sur Juda*, Aix-en-Provence, Archives Nationales Section Outre-Mer, DFC 75, pièce 112, 57 p.

AZONAHA Dossou Jonas, 2024, *Histoire des migrations maxi vers Atakpamé: XVIIIe-XIXe siècles*, Lomé, Les Éditions Le Plaisir, 154 p.

BACQUELAINE Daniel, WILLEMS Ferdy and COENEN Marie-Thérèse, 2001, *Enquête parlementaire visant à déterminer les circonstances exactes de l'assassinat de Patrice Lumumba et l'implication éventuelle des responsables politiques belges dans celui-ci, Chambre des représentants de Belgique*, vol. 2, 988 p.

BAUDRY des LOZIÈRES, 1893, *Second voyage à la Louisiane, faisant suite au premier de l'auteur, de 1794 à 1798*, Paris, Chez Charles, t. 2, 410 p.

BAY Edna G., 1998, *Wives of the Leopard: Gender, politics and culture in the Kingdom of Dahomey*, Charlottesville & London, University of Virginia Press, 376 p.

BÉART Ch., 1955, *Jeux et jouets de l'Ouest africain*, Dakar, IFAN, t. 2, 888 p.

BERBAIN Simone, 1942, *Études sur la traite des noirs au Golfe de Guinée: le comptoir français de Juda (Ouidah) au XVIIIe siècle*, Paris, Larose, 125 p.

BERGOUGNIOU Jean-Michel, CLIGNET Rémi and DAVID Philippe, 2001, *« Villages Noirs » et visiteurs africains et malgaches en France et en Europe (1870-1940)*, Paris, Karthala, 303 p.

BOUCHE Abbé Pierre, 1885, *Sept ans en Afrique Occidentale: la côte des Esclaves et le Dahomey*, Paris, E. Plon, Nourrit et Cie, 403 p.

BOUILLON Antoine and ARCHER Robert, 1981, *Le sport et l'apartheid: sous le maillot, la race*, Paris, Editons Albatros, 319 p

BRUNET Louis and GIETHLEN L., 1900, *Dahomey et dépendances*, Paris, A. Challamel, 544 p.

CALMET Dom Augustin, 1722, *Dictionnaire historique, critique, chronologique, géographique et littéral de la Bible, enrichi d'un grand nombre de figures en taille douce, qui représentent les Antiquités judaïques*, Paris, Saugrain, t. 1, 568 p.

CANDOLLE Alphonse de, 1886, *Origine des plantes cultivées*, Paris, Félix Alcan, 3e édition, 385 p.

CHANDON de BRIAILLES Jean-Remy, 1902, *Les colonies françaises: leur présent, leur avenir, conférence faite le 21 mai 1902*, cercle d'instruction populaire d'Epernay, 62 p.

CHEVAL Alexia, 2022, *Pourquoi le rire est-il un atout pour le bien-être? Les bienfaits scientifiques prouvés*, Bruxelles, Institute of NeuroCognitivism, 7 p.

CISSÉ Daniel Amara, 1988, *Histoire économique de l'Afrique noire. L'économie des origines: du Néolithique à l'Antiquité (-12 millions d'années à −3000 avant notre ère)*, Abidjan/Paris, PUSAF/L'Harmattan, 223 p.

CLAPARÈDE (Dr.), 1861, *La circoncision. De son importance dans la famille et dans l'Etat*, Paris, chez l'auteur, 25 p.

COQUERY-VIDROVITCH Catherine, 2021, *Les routes de l'esclavage. Histoire des traites africaines, VIe-XXe siècle*, Paris, Albin Michel, 312 p.

COQUERY-VIDROVITCH Catherine and MESNARD Éric, 2019, *Être esclave. Afrique-Amériques, XVe-XIXe siècle*, Paris, Paris, La Découverte, 335 p.

COQUERY-VIDROVITCH Catherine, 2016, *Petite histoire de l'Afrique. L'Afrique au sud du Sahara, de la préhistoire à nos jours*, Paris, La Découverte, 226 p.

d'ALBÉCA A. L., 1895, *La France au Dahomey*, Paris, Librairie Hachette et Cie, 236 p.

DALZEL Archibald, 1793, *The history of Dahomy, an inland Kingdom of Africa*, Londres, 230 p.

DAPPER Olfert, 1686, *Description de l'Afrique*, Amsterdam, W. Waesberge, Boom & Van Someren, VI-534 p.

de MEDEIROS François, 1985, *L'Occident et l'Afrique (XIIIe-XVe siècle)*, Paris, Karthala, 305 p.

de SOUZA Simonne, 1992, *La famille de Souza. Bénin-Togo*, Cotonou, Les Éditions du Bénin, 322 p.

DESPLANTES Fr., 1894, *Le général Dodds et l'expédition du Dahomey*, Rouen, Mégard et Cie, 224 p.

DIAKITÉ Tidiane, 2008, *La traite des Noirs et ses acteurs africains*, Paris, Berg International Éditeurs, 238 p.

DIOP Cheikh Anta, 1979, *Nations nègres et culture*, Paris, Présence africaine, 564 p.

DJIVO Joseph Adrien, 2013, *Le refus de la colonisation dans l'ancien royaume de Danxomè (1875-1894): Gbèhanzin et Ago-li-Agbo*, Paris, L'Harmattan, vol. 1, 418 p.

FOÁ Édouard, 1895, *Le Dahomey: histoire, géographie, mœurs, coutumes, industrie, expéditions françaises (1891-1894)*, Paris, A. Hennuyer, 430 p.

FONDATION DE LA MÉMOIRE DE L'ESCLAVAGE, 2023, *Les Notes de la FME*, Paris, Fondation de la mémoire de l'esclavage, n° 3, 27 p.

GARCIA Luc, 1988, *Le royaume du Dahomé face à la pénétration coloniale (1875-1894)*, Paris, Karthala, 284 p.

GAYIBOR Nicoué (under the direction of), 2011, *Histoire des Togolais: des origines aux années 1960. Du XVIe siècle à l'occupation coloniale*, Paris/Lomé, Karthala/Presses de l'UL, tome 2, 715 p.

GAYIBOR Nicoué Lodjou, 1990, *Le Genyi: un royaume oublié de la Côte de Guinée au temps de la traite des Noirs*, Lomé, Editions Haho, 321 p.

HAZOUMÉ Paul, 1956, *Le pacte de sang au Dahomey*, Paris, Institut d'Ethnologie, 170 p.

HOUÉNOUDÉ Didier Marcel, 2009, *Musique traditionnelle à Abomey*, Lomé, Imprimerie IPACOM, 49 p.

IBN KHALDOUN, 2006, *Les prolégomènes*, Chicoutimi, Bibliothèque Paul-Émile Boulet de l'Université du Québec, t. 1, 436 p.

KANE Ousmane, 2003, *Intellectuels non europhones*, Dakar, Codesria, 71 p.

KHALID Khalid Mohammad, 2010, *Des hommes autour du prophète (Qu'Allah le bénisse et le salue)*, Beyrouth, Dar Al-Kotob Al-llmiyah, 319 p.

KI-ZERBO Joseph, 2003, *À quand l'Afrique? Entretien avec René Holenstein*, Cotonou, Éditions Ruisseaux d'Afrique, 197 p.

LABAT Jean-Baptiste, 1730, *Voyage du chevalier Des Marchais en Guinée, isles voisines et à Cayenne, fait en 1725, 1726 et 1727*, Paris, Saugrin, vol. 2, 364 p.

MAIREAU Roma, BOUCETTA Nadia and LANGLOIS Brice, 2017, « *La musique sous Louis XVI* »: Le 13ᵉ piano de *Marie-Antoinette?*, Tours, Université François-Rabelais, 18 p.

Mc LEOD John M. D., 1820, *A voyage to Africa, with some account of the manners and customs of the Dahomian people*, London, John Murray, 162 p.

MEHAZZEM Allah, 2025, *Histoire des mathématiques*, Mila, Centre universitaire Abdelhafidh Boussouf/ Institut de Mathématiques et informatique, 44 p.

MURDOCK George Peter, 1969, *Africa. Its peoples and their culture history*, New-York, McGraw-Hill Book, 456 p.

N'DIAYE Tidiane, 2008, *Le génocide voilé: enquête historique*, Paris, Gallimard, 253 p.

NLANDU NGUNDA Jean, 2024, *Histoire et épistémologie de l'informatique. Licence. Histoire et épistémologie de l'informatique*, Kinshasa, ISP Mbanza-Ngungu, 65 p.

NORRIS Robert, 1790, *Mémoire du règne de Bossa Ahadée, roi de Dahomé, État situé à l'intérieur de la Guinée et voyage de l'auteur à Abomé qui en est la capitale*, Paris, Gattey, 243 p.

OLIVEIRA MARQUES A. H. de, 1998, *Histoire du Portugal et de son empire colonial*, Paris, Karthala, 615 p.

POIRIER Jules, 1896, *Campagne du Dahomey: 1892-1894. Précédée d'une étude géographique et historique sur ce pays et suivie de la carte au 1/5000000ᵉ établie au bureau topographique de l'État-major du corps expéditionnaire par ordre de Mr. Le Général Dodds (1895)*, Paris, Limoges, Henri Charles- Lavauzelle, 370 p.

QUENUM Alphonse, 1993, *Les Églises chrétiennes et la traite atlantique du XVe au XIXe siècle*, Paris, Karthala, 341 p.

SAVARIAU Nicolas, 1906, *L'agriculture au Dahomey*, Paris, A. Challamel, 110 p.

SKERTCHLY J. Alfred, 1874, *Dahomey as it is: being a narrative of eight months residence in that country*, London, Chapman and Hall, Piccadilly, 524 p.

SMITH Guillaume, 1751, *Nouveau voyage de Guinée*, Paris, Durand & Pessot, 2 vols, 571 p.

SNELGRAVE G., 2008, *Journal d'un négrier au XVIIIe siècle: nouvelle relation de quelques endroits de Guinée et du commerce d'esclaves qu'on y fait*, Paris, Gallimard, 254 p.

SNELGRAVE Guillaume, 1735, *Nouvelle relation de quelques endroits de Guinée et du commerce d'esclaves qu'on y fait*, Amsterdam, 348 p.

TOURTE René, 2005, *Histoire de la recherche agricole en Afrique tropicale francophone*, Rome, FAO, 132 p.

THURAM Lilian, 2014, *Mes étoiles noires: de Lucy à Barack Obama*, Cotonou, Ruisseaux d'Afrique, 400 p.

VANDENBERG Philipp, 1977, *Ramsès II*, Paris, Pierre Belfond, 316 p.

VERGER Pierre, 1968, *Flux et reflux de la traite des nègres entre le golfe de Bénin et Bahia de todos os Santos du dix-septième au dix-neuvième siècle*, Paris, Mouton, 720 p.

VIDO Agossou Arthur and VIDO Codjo Marius, 2025, *Les femmes dans l'histoire du Bas-Bénin (XVIIe-XIXe siècles)*, Abomey, Éditions Naguézé, 253 p.

VIDO Agossou Arthur, YOBOUÉ Yao Serge and AZONHÈ Thierry, 2024, *Les Fon à travers les écrits d'auteurs béninois: 229 références bibliographiques pour une meilleure connaissance du patrimoine historique d'une communauté multiculturelle*, Abomey, Éditions Naguézé, 327 p.

VIDO Arthur, 2019, *Biographie du roi Kpengla du Danhomè (1774-1789)*, Paris, L'Harmattan, 170 p.

VIDO Arthur, 2014, *L'histoire du riz africain dans le Sud-Bénin (XVIIe-XXe siècle): une contribution à l'étude de l'histoire rurale du Bénin*, Sarrebruck, Presses Académiques Francophones, 355 p.

WATCH TOWER BIBLE AND TRACT SOCIETY, 1997, *Étude perspicace des Écritures*, Brooklyn, New York, Watch Tower Bible and Tract Society of New York, 2 vols, 2554 p.

WAUTIER André, *Dictionnaire des gnostiques et des principaux initiés*, 278 p. Cf. chrome-extension:// efaidnbmnnnibpcajpcglclefind-mkaj/http://www. theologica.fr/! Diction-naires/Dictionnaires-%20Encyclopedies.%20 Ertc/Wautier%20Andr%C3%A9%20-%20 Dic-tionnaire%20des%20gnostiques%20et%20des %20principaux%20initi%C3%A9s.pdf. Visité le 3 janvier 2026 à 11 heures 41 minutes.

ZOHOU Arnaud, 2021, *Une histoire du Vodoun: l'acte de vivre*, Paris, Présence Africaine, 271 p.

ZÖLLER Hugo, 1990, *Le Togo en 1884 selon Hugo Zöller*, translated by A. Amegan and A. Ahadji, Lomé, Éditions Haho/Orstom, 216 p.

Articles

ADANDÉ Alexis B. A., 1993, « Les origines loin-taines des peuples de la République du Bénin: problématique et perspectives de recherches », *Afrika Zamani*, Nouvelle série n° 1, p. 65-92.

ADJA Kouassi, 2016, « Malam Musa: un colon nègre (un colon pas comme les autres) », *Re-vue du Groupe d'Études et de Recherches Afri-caines et Hispano-Américaines*, n° 2, p. 4-22.

ADJIVÈSSODÉ Patrick Joël, 2016, « Pouvoir royal et instances de régulation au Danhomè », *in*

Yao Marcel Kouakou, Didier Marcel Houénoudé, Agossou Arthur Vido and Romuald Tchibozo (under the direction of), *Regards sur l'histoire politique de l'Afrique noire d'hier à nos jours*, Saint-Denis, Edilivre, p. 41-55.

ADOTÉVI L. Senyon, 1999, « Les Ifê de la région d'Atakpamé des origines à 1884 », *in* T. Gbeasor (under the direction of), *Espace, culture et développement dans la région d'Atakpamé*, Actes du colloque « Atakpamé: Espace et Civilisation » (10-12 décembre 1997), Lomé, Presses de l'UB, p. 5-38.

ADOTÉVI A. S. Louis, 1996, « Les Fon-Mahi de la région d'Atakpamé des origines à 1884 », *Annales de l'Université du Bénin*, Série Lettres, t. XVI, p. 129-177.

AKODIGNA Achéssi Magloire and VIDO Agossou Arthur, 2017, « La divinité Ogou dans le panthéon idaatcha: une contribution à l'histoire des religions endogènes de l'aire culturelle yoruba », *in* Agossou Arthur Vido and Paul Akogni (under the direction of), *Regards croisés sur l'histoire et le patrimoine culturels africains à l'aube du 21ᵉ siècle*, Saint-Denis, Edilivre, p. 51-66.

ARAUJO Ana Lucia, 2014, « La correspondance du roi Adandozan avec la couronne portugaise: petite histoire d'une grande amitié », *in* Guy Saupin (under the direction of), *Africains et Européens dans le monde atlantique (XVᵉ-XIXᵉ siècle)*, Rennes, Presses Universitaires de Rennes, p. 129-151.

BINET Édouard, 1900, « Observations sur les Dahoméens », *Bulletins de la Société d'Anthropologie de Paris*, 5ᵉ Série, tome 1, p. 244-253.

BOËTSCH Gilles, 2011, « Georges Cuvier, un nouveau regard sur le monde », *in* Pascal blanchard, Gilles boëtsch and Nanette Jacomijn snoep (under the direction of), *Exhibitions. L'invention du sauvage*, Paris, Actes Sud/Musée du quai Branly, p. 64.

BON François and FAUVELLE François-Xavier, 2022, « Les archives africaines du monde: empreintes, fossiles, vestiges, langues et récits de la préhistoire », *in* François-Xavier Fauvelle and Anne Lafont (under the direction of), *L'Afrique et le monde: histoires renouées, de la Préhistoire au XXIᵉ siècle*, Paris, La Découverte, p. 17-43.

BOSCO Kalame Iyamuse, 1989, « Chaka, la légende vivante », *Le Courrier de l'Unesco*, XLII, 9, p. 44-47.

BRAUDE Benjamin, 2002, « Cham et Noé. Race, esclavage et exégèse entre islam, judaïsme et christianisme », *Annales, Histoire et sciences sociales*, n° 1, p. 93-125.

CALLOT Valérie, 2023, « Peau noire et dermatologie: une histoire récente », *Histoire des sciences médicales*, tome V, p. 175-184.

CAPONE Stefania, 2018, « Le troisième élément ou les mathématiques morales d'Ifá », *L'Homme*, n° 225, p. 171-184.

CARNEY Judith, 2005, « Rice and memory in the age of enslavement: Atlantic passages to Suriname », *Slavery and abolition*, vol. 26, n° 3, p. 325-347.

CARNEY Judith, 2001, « African rice in the Columbian exchange », *The Journal of African History*, vol. 42, n° 3, p. 377-396.

CASTELLO BRANCO Garcia Mendes, 1881, « Da Mina ao Cabo negro », *in* L. Cordeiro (texts gathered by), *Viagens e explorações e conquistas dos Portugueses (1574-1620)*, Lisboa, Imprensa Nacional, p. 7-33.

CHARLES Pierre (s.j.), 1928, « Les noirs, fils de Cham le maudit », *Nouvelle revue théologique*, 55, n° 10, p. 721-739.

CHEMILLIER Marc, 2008, « Éléments pour une ethnomathématique de l'awélé », *Mathématiques et sciences humaines*, n° 181, p. 5-33.

CHEVALIER Augustin, 1936, « L'importance de la riziculture dans le domaine colonial français et l'orientation à donner aux recherches agricoles », *Laboratoire d'agronomie coloniale*, p. 27-45.

CISSOKO Sékéné Mody, 1969, « L'intelligentsia de Tombouctou aux XVe et XVIe siècles », *Présence africaine*, n° 72, p. 48-72.

CLARK Desmond, 1962, « The spread of food production in subsaharian Africa », *Journal of African History*, III (2), p. 211-228.

da CRUZ Clément, 1954, « Les instruments de musique dans le Bas-Dahomey (populations Fon, Adja, Kotafon, Péda, Aïzo) », *Études Dahoméennes*, XII, IFAN, 79 p. + 20 planches.

DIOP Cheikh Anta, 1980, « Origine des anciens Egyptiens », *in* G. Mokhtar (under the direction of), *Histoire générale de l'Afrique*, Paris, Jeune Afrique-Editions Stock-Unesco, vol. 2, p. 40-74.

DORGÈRE R. P., 1955, « Prisonniers de Béhanzin », *L'Almanach Noir*, p. 9-16.

DUNGLAS Édouard, 1957, « Contribution à l'histoire du moyen-Dahomey (royaumes d'Abomey, de Kétou et de Ouidah) (suite) », *Études Dahoméennes*, tome II, XX, 152 p.

ELOM-NTOUZO'O E., 1978, « Médecine, pharmacopées traditionnelles et développement en Afrique », *Présence africaine*, n° 108, p. 38-49.

FALCON P., 1954, « La reddition de Béhanzin, roi du Dahomey », *L'Almanach Noir*, p. 15-20.

FORTIN Sylvie, TRUDELLE Sylvie and RAIL Geneviève, 2008, « Incorporation paradoxale des normes esthétiques et de santé chez les danseurs contemporains », *in* Sylvie Fortin (under the direction of), *Danse et santé: du corps intime au corps social*, Québec, Presses de l'Université du Québec, p. 9-44.

GNAGNY Pedro Kennedy, 2023, « L'héroïsme épique arabe en question dans Antara de Marce Devic; entre epicisme et courtoise chevaleresque », *Akofena*, Hors-série n° 03, p. 163-174.

GNAMMANKOU Dieudonné, 2008, « La diaspora africaine en Europe: de l'Antiquité à la fin du XIXe siècle », *in* Dieudonné Gnammankou and Yao Modzinou (under the direction of), *Les Africains et leurs descendants en Europe avant le XXe siècle*, Toulouse MAT Éditions, p. 51-69.

GUÉZO Anselme, 2010, « Langage et objectivité historique: une approche critique du discours ethnographique dans l'historiographie du Danxomè », *Annales de la Faculté des Lettres, Arts et Sciences Humaines Université d'Abomey-Calavi (Benin)*, vol. 1, n° 16, p. 75-100.

HARDY Jean-Pierre and CASTÉRAN Nicole, 2002, « L'hygiène personnelle dans la vallée du Saint-Laurent, 1790-1835 », *Cap-aux-Diamants, La revue d'histoire du Québec*, n° 70, p. 10-13.

HENRY Christine, 2008, « Le sorcier, le visionnaire et la guerre des Églises au Sud-Bénin », *Cahiers d'Études africaines*, XLVIII (1-2), 189-190, p. 101-130.

HUJESON Pierre-Claver, 1952, « Pourquoi y a-t-il Blancs et pourquoi des Noirs? Récit légendaire d'un aïeul Noir à ses petits enfants », *L'Almanach noir*, p. 39-41.

IGUÉ John O., 2009, « Le rôle de la colonisation dans l' "immobilisme" des sociétés africaines », *in* Adame Ba Konaré (under the direction of), *Petit précis de remise à niveau sur l'histoire africaine à l'usage du président Sarkozy*, Paris, La Découverte, p. 215-226.

IROKO Abiola Félix, 2025, « Roi, blessés de guerre et guérisseurs dans le Danxomè (XVIIIe-XIXe

s) », *in* Agossou Arthur Vido (under the direction of), *Les royaumes d'Alada et du Danxomè à l'épreuve du temps. Quelques éclairages historiques sur deux cités des descendants d'Adjahouto*, Abomey, Les Éditions Naguézé, p. 105-110.

IROKO Abiola Félix, VIDO Arthur and ATCHAMOU Christelle, 2019, « Le rôle du *Kpamègan* dans la politique sanitaire du Danhomè », *in* Paul Akogni, Arthur Vido and Didier Marcel Houénoudé (under the direction of), *Le patrimoine historique au service du développement du Bénin*, Paris, L'Harmattan, p. 91-100.

IROKO Abiola Félix, 2002, « Aspects de la politique sanitaire des rois du Danhomè (suite et fin) », *La croix du Bénin*, p. 4.

KAKPO Mahougnon, 2021, « Le fa comme vecteur de savoirs littéraires », *in* Musanji Nglasso-Mwatha (under the direction of), *Littératures, savoirs et enseignement*, Pessac, Presses Universitaires de Bordeaux, p. 165-175.

KLEIN Herbert S. and ENGERMAN Stanley L., 1976, « Facteurs de mortalité dans le trafic français d'esclaves au XVIIIe siècle », *Annales. Economies, Sociétés, Civilisations*, n° 6, p. 1213-1224.

KOUDJO Bienvenu, 2005, « Glèlè le musicien-chorégraphe: la musique et la danse comme outils d'historicisation au Danxomè », *in* Elisée Soumonni (under the coordination of), *Centenaire de la mort du roi Glèlè (1889-1989). Actes du colloque international sur la vie et l'œuvre du roi Glèlè (1858-1889). Abomey, 27-29 décembre 1989*, Cotonou, Association pour la sauvegarde du patrimoine du roi Glèlè, 17 p.

KOUDJO Bienvenu, 1988, « Parole et musique chez les Fon et les Gun du Bénin: pour une nouvelle taxinomie de la parole littéraire », *Journal des africanistes*, tome 58, fascicule 2. p. 73-97.

LAGARDÈRE Vincent, 1996, « La riziculture en al-Andalus (VIIIe –XVe siècles) », *Studia Islamica*, n° 83, p. 71-87.

L'ALMANACH NOIR, 1938, « Nos primitifs et la maladie », *L'Almanach noir*, p. 59-61.

LOMBARD Jacques, 1967, « Pensée politique et démocratie dans l'Afrique noire traditionnelle », *Présence Africaine*, n° 63, p. 10-31.

MAHÉ A., 2015, « Dermatologie des peaux dites "noires" », *EMC – Dermatologie*, vol 10, n° 4, p. 1-9.

MANNING Patrick, 1993, « Structure économique et politique économique dans l'histoire du Bénin », *Afrika Zamani*, Nouvelle série n° 1, p. 163-173.

MODZINOU Yao, 2008, « Notes préliminaires », *in* Dieudonné Gnammankou and Yao Modzinou (under the direction of), *Les Africains et leurs descendants en Europe avant le XXe siècle*, Toulouse MAT Éditions, p. 17-30.

MONDJANNAGNI Alfred, 1969, « Contribution à l'étude des paysages végétaux du bas-Dahomey », *Annales de l'Université d 'Abidjan*, série G, I (2), 191 p.

MUNSON Patrick. J., 1976, « Archaeological data on the origins of cultivation in the southwestern Sahara and their implications for West Africa », *in* Jack Rodney Harlan, Jan M. J. de Wett and Ann Stemler (eds.), *Origins of African plant domestication*, The Hargue, Mouton, p. 187-209.

N'TIA Roger, 1993, « Géopolitique de l'Atakora précolonial », *Afrika Zamani*, Revue annuelle d'histoire africaine, Nouvelle série, n° 1, p. 107-124.

OBENGA Mwene Ndzale, 1969, « L'Afrique dans l'Antiquité », *Présence africaine*, n° 72, p. 73-84.

OBICHERE Boniface I., 1978, « Women and Slavery in the Kingdom of Dahomey », *Revue française d'Histoire d'outre-mer*, t. 65, n° 238, p. 5-20.

PÉROUSE DE MONTCLOS Marc-Antoine, 2002, « Les esclaves invisibles de l'Islam: à quand l'heure de la vérité? », *Etudes*, tome 396, n° 3966, p. 751-759.

PIÉTRI Camille-N., 1890, « Nos 93 jours de captivité au Dahomé », *Journal des voyages*, t. 26-27, n° 702, p. 385-400.

PORTÈRES Roland and BARRAU Jacques, 1980, « Début, développement et expansion des techniques agricoles », *in* Joseph Ki-Zerbo (under the direction of), *Histoire générale de l'Afrique*, Paris, Jeune-Afrique-Editons Stock-UNESCO, vol. 1, p. 725-744.

PURSEGLOVE J. W., 1976, « The origins and migrations of crops in tropical Africa », *in* Jack Rodney Harlan, Jan M. J. de Wett and Ann Stemler (eds.), *Origins of African plant domestication*, The Hargue, Mouton, p. 291-307.

QUENUM Maximilien, 1935, « Au pays des Fons », *Bulletin du comité d'études historiques et scientifiques de l'Afrique occidentale française*, tome XVIII, p. 141-335.

RILLY Claude, 2017, « Les fils royaux de Koush: colonisation égyptienne. 1450-850 av. J.-C. », *in* Olivier Cabon (under the direction of), *Histoire et civilisation du Soudan: de la préhistoire à nos jours*, Paris, Africae, p. 87-114.

RUDERMAN Anne, 2022, « Formation d'un monde, l'Atlantique: marché africain, marché global (XVe-XIXe siècle) », *in* François-Xavier Fauvelle and Anne Lafont (under the direction of), *L'Afrique et le monde: histoires renouées, de la Préhistoire au XXIe siècle*, Paris, La Découverte, p. 91-122.

SADAI Célia, 2021, « Racisme anti-Noirs au Maghreb: dévoilement(s) d'un tabou », *Hérodote*, n° 180, p. 131-148.

SAVY Nicole, 2015, « Le racisme à travers l'histoire: choses, mots et idées », *Hommes et Libertés*, n° 172, p. 35-38.

SOLOUM Salomé and GOMINA Abdou Gafarou, 2022, « Les instruments de musique dans l'histoire des populations du Sud-Bénin (XVIIe-XIXe siècles) », *in* Arthur Vido, Richard Gouédan Meignan and Mamadou Yéro Baldé (under the direction of), *Héritages culturels et formes de pensées en Afrique de l'Ouest (XVe-XXIe siècles): identités et mutations au Bénin, en Côte d'Ivoire et au Sénégal*, Surgeon Falls Ontario (Canada), Éditions AB Alkebulan, p. 90-103.

TIDJANI-SERPOS Nouréïni, 1975, « L'appareil idéologique colonial scolaire de la France en Afrique », *Annales*, n° 1, p. 102-106.

VALLON Auguste, 1861, « Le royaume de Daho-mey (Fin) », *Revue maritime et coloniale*, t. III, octobre, p. 329-358.

VERGER Pierre, 1969, « Relations commerciales et culturelles entre le Brésil et le Golfe du Bé-nin », *Journal de la Société des Africanistes*, t. 58, p. 35-56.

VERGER Pierre, 1968, « Les côtes d'Afrique Occi-dentale entre "Rio Volta" et "Rio Lagos" (1535-1773) », *Journal de la Société des Afri-canistes*, vol. 38, n° 1, p. 35-58.

VERGER Pierre, 1965, « Le fort portugais de Oui-dah (première partie) », *Études Dahoméennes*, nouvelle série, n° 4, p. 5-50.

VIDO Agossou Arthur and KOUASSI Kouassi Raguin, 2025, « La circoncision dans l'histoire des peuples du golfe du Bénin (XVIe-XIXe siè-cles) », *Les cahiers du LARSOC (CDL)*, vol. 2, n° 1, p. 160-178.

VIDO Marius and VIDO Arthur, 2022, « Une étude sur les divertissements des rois du Danx-omè (XVIIe-XIXe siècles) », *in* Arthur Vido, Richard Gouédan Meignan and Mamadou Yéro Baldé (under the direction of), *Héritages* culturels et formes de pensées en Afrique de l'Ouest (XVe-XXIe siècles): identités et mutations au Bénin, en Côte d'Ivoire et au Sénégal, Surgeon Falls Ontario (Canada), Éditions AB Alkebulan, p. 104-118.

VIDO Marius and VIDO Arthur, 2022, « L'ingratitude et la trahison dans l'histoire du Danxomè: le cas de Juliao Félix de Souza (1832-1887) », *in* Arthur Vido, Richard Gouédan Meignan and Mamadou Yéro Baldé (under the direction of), *Héritages culturels et formes de pensées en Afrique de l'Ouest (XVe-XXIe siècles): identités et mutations au Bénin, en Côte d'Ivoire et au Sénégal*, Surgeon Falls Ontario (Canada), Éditions AB Alkebulan, p. 151-162.

VIDO Arthur, 2021a, « Les découvertes archéologiques sur l'espèce *Oryza glaberrima* Steudel ou la mise en question de l'approche "indirecte" de l'archéologie élaborée par Roland Portères pour dater la riziculture africaine à plus de 3500 ans d'existence », *Annales de la FASHS*, vol. 2, n° 004, p. 111-118.

VIDO Arthur, 2021b, « Biographie d'Assou, un haut dignitaire du royaume de Sahé (1704-1733) », *Uirtus*, vol. 1, n° 2, p. 487-501.

VIDO Agossou Arthur, 2015, « La diffusion du riz africain (*Oryza glaberrima* Steudel) en Afrique du Nord, du Centre, de l'Est, en Europe et en Asie: essai d'analyse historique », *in* Brice Sinsin, Flavien Gbéto and Brice Tenté (under the direction of), *Mélanges Jean Pliya*, Cotonou, Imprimerie COPEF, p. 287-296.

VOGT John L., 1973, « The early Sao Tome-Principe Slave Trade with Mina, 1500-1540 », *The international journal of African historical studies*, vol. 6, n° 3, p. 453-464.

VYCICHL Werner, 1957, « Le pays de Koush dans une inscription éthiopienne », *Annales d' Éthiopie*, vol. 2, p. 177-179.

WHITFORD David M., 2021, « La disparition de Canaan: malédiction de Cham et justifications de l'esclavage à l'époque moderne », *Revue d'histoire moderne et contemporaine*, 68-2, p. 79-103.

ZABOROWSKI Sigismond, 1893, « Origine des plantes cultivées et de la culture dans l'Afrique noire. Usages et peuples de l'Afrique occidentale: les Sabangas », *Bulletins de la Société d'anthropologie de Paris*, IVᵉ Série, tome 4, p. 508-532.

ZYLBERMAN Patrick, 2017, « L'intestin de la grande ville: es égouts et l'hygiène à Paris à la fin du XIXᵉ siècle », *Les tribunes de la santé*, n° 56, p. 21-28.

Dissertations and theses

ADJIVÈSSODÉ Patrick Joël, 2015, *La question des droits de la personne humaine en Afrique sub-saharienne précoloniale: le cas du Danxomɛ des origines à l'occupation française*, PhD thesis in History, University of Abomey-Calavi, 316 p.

AGOSSOU Ahogla, 2007, *Monographie du village de Sada: début XIXᵉ siècle à nos jours*, Master's thesis in History, University of Lomé, 85 p.

ARAUJO Ana Lucia, 2007, *Mémoires de l'esclavage et de la traite des esclaves dans l'Atlantique sud: enjeux de la patrimonialisation au Brésil et au Bénin*, PhD thesis in History, Laval University Quebec, 368 p.

ASSOGBA Tognon, 2006, *Contribution à l'histoire des Fon-Mahi du Togo: étude monographique du canton d'Atchinédji du début XIXᵉ siècle à 1990*, Master's thesis in History, University of Lomé, 94 p.

ATTIVI Kokou, 2007, *Les chefferies traditionnelles (chefs temporel et spirituel) en milieu ifè: cas de Tchetti (GNAGNA) d'Atakpamé de la fin du XVIIIᵉ siècle à 2000*, Master's thesis in History, University of Lomé, 97 p.

CAUSSIN François, 2016, *Musiques et musiciens à Grenoble au XVIIᵉ siècle (1590-1730)*, Master's thesis 2 « Human and social sciences », Grenoble Alpes University, 231 p.

CISSOKO Mahamadou, 2019, *Les relations afro-maghrébines du foyer au quartier. La fraternité islamique à l'épreuve du quotidien*, PhD thesis in Sociology, University of Paris VIII, 353 p.

COSTES Victor, 2020, *Le XVIIIe siècle: naissance de l'odontologie moderne en France*, thesis for the state diploma of Doctor in Dental Surgery, University of Paris, 63 p.

DÈGBÈLO Amélie, 1993, *Traitement de la maladie dans le royaume du Danxomè aux XVIIIe et XIXe siècles*, thesis with a view to obtaining the Doctorate (New Regime), University of Paris 1 Panthéon-Sorbonne, 2 volumes, 779 p + Annexes.

DOSSOU Adivignon, 2007, *Contribution à l'histoire du peuplement de la région d'Atakpamé: Gléi du début du XIXe siècle à 1960*, Master's thesis in History, University of Lomé, 69 p.

GLÉSSOUGBÉ Théodore, 2012, *Une étude historique du rythme « Zɛnli » dans le Bas-Bénin précolonial*, Master's thesis in History, University of Abomey-Calavi, 78 p.

GOSSIAUX Axel Mudahemuka, 2022, *La persistance des stéréotypes issus de la propagande co-*

loniale: comment le passé colonial explique le racisme contemporain en Belgique, report, Centre for the Study of Ethnicity and Migration (CEDEM)/Faculty of Social Sciences (FaSS) - Institute for Research in Social Sciences (IRSS)/University of Liège (ULiège), 77 p.

HENNEQUIN Pascal, 2001, *Santé et hygiène de l'enfant dans l'Égypte ancienne*, thesis to obtain the degree of Doctor of Medicine, Henri Poincaré University, Nancy 1, 263 p.

HODONOU Félix F., 1989, *Jeux et loisirs traditionnels au Sud de la République populaire du Bénin: le cas de la province de l'Atlantique*, Master's thesis in Sociology-Anthropology, National University of Benin, 158 p. + Annexes.

KOSSOU Sovi, 2017, *Les communautés ifè de la région d'Atakpamé: du XVIIᵉ siècle à 1914*, PhD thesis in History, University of Lomé, 424 p.

KOUNKOUAGA CHABI T. M., 2003, *Société traditionnelle et démocratie: les formes d'expression de la démocratie chez les Natimba de l'Atakora précolonial*, Master's thesis in History, University of Abomey Calavi, 82 p.

LAINÉ Agnès, 1998, *Génétique des populations et histoire du peuplement de l'Afrique. Essai d'historiographie et d'épistémologie*, thesis to obtain the degree of Doctor from the University Paris 1, 2 tomes.

ODAH Toutou Komi Akomangni, 2021, *La diaspora Kabiyè dans la région d'Atakpamé au Sud-Togo aux XIXe et XXe siècles*, Master's thesis in History, University of Lomé, 93 p.

OLOUGBÉGNON Dossou Ogoutchina, 2016, *Les Idatcha (Bénin -Togo), de la fin du XVe siècle à la conquête coloniale européenne*, PhD thesis in History, University of Lomé, 611 p.

ÖZKORAY Hayri Gökşin, 2017, *L'esclavage dans l'Empire ottoman (XVIe-XVIIe siècle): fondements juridiques, réalités socio-économiques, représentations*, PhD thesis from the Research University Paris Sciences and Letters, 776 p.

PALAU MARTI Montserrat, 1960, *Essai sur la notion de roi chez les Yoruba et les Aja-Fon (Nigeria et Dahomey)*, postgraduate thesis, University of Paris, 259 p.

PASQUINI Aude, 2002, *Evolution de l'hygiène bucco-dentaire au fil des siècles et des civilisations*, thesis for the Doctorate in dental surgery, Henri Poincaré University, Nancy 1, 291 p.

SAVARY Claude, 1976, *La pensée symbolique des Fö du Dahomey: tableau de la société et étude de la littérature orale d'expression sacrée dans l'ancien royaume du Dahomey*, PhD thesis, University of Neuchâtel, Geneva, Editions Medicine and hygiene, 396 p.

TIANDO Emmanuel, 1978, *Perspectives d'approche historique des populations de l'Atakora. L'exemple des Waaba – Tangamba – Daataba*, Master's thesis in History, National University of Benin, 207 p.

VARISSOU Souayibou, 1992, *Un aspect de l'histoire rurale dans le Sud-Bénin: l'introduction du maïs et son impact dans les activités agraires du XVIe au XIXe siècle*, Master's thesis in History, National University of Benin, 114 p.

Table of contents

Editorial coordination: Satingo Ricardo Kissoe
Site: www.kondopress.com
Email: info@kondopress.com
Tel: +1 (763) 202-8400
Minneapolis, Minnesota (USA)
Address: 202 N Cedar Ave Ste #1, Owatonna, MN 55060 US